NOTES

ON THE

FLORIDIAN PENINSULA,

ITS

LITERARY HISTORY,

INDIAN TRIBES AND ANTIQUITIES.

BY

DANIEL G. BRINTON, A. B.

PHILADELPHIA:
PUBLISHED BY JOSEPH SABIN,
No. 27 South Sixth Street, above Chestnut.
1859.

KING & BAIRD, PRINTERS, PHILADA.

TO THE

LOVERS AND CULTIVATORS

OF THE

HISTORY AND ARCHÆOLOGY OF OUR COUNTRY,

THIS WORK

IS RESPECTFULLY DEDICATED,

BY THE AUTHOR.

PREFACE.

The present little work is the partial result of odd hours spent in the study of the history, especially the ancient history—if by this term I may be allowed to mean all that pertains to the aborigines and first settlers—of the peninsula of Florida. In some instances, personal observations during a visit thither, undertaken for the purposes of health in the winter of 1856–57, have furnished original matter, and served to explain, modify, or confirm the statements of previous writers.

Aware of the isolated interest ever attached to merely local history, I have endeavored, as far as possible, by pointing out various analogies, and connecting detached facts, to impress upon it a character of general value to the archæologist and historian. Should the attempt have been successful, and should the book aid as an incentive to the rapidly increasing attention devoted to subjects of this nature, I shall feel myself amply repaid for the hours of toil, which have also ever been hours of pleasure, spent in its preparation.

Thornbury, Penna., April, 1859.

CONTENTS.

CHAPTER I.

LITERARY HISTORY.

CHAPTER II.

THE APALACHES.

CHAPTER III.

TRIBES OF THE SIXTEENTH CENTURY.

CHAPTER IV.

LATER TRIBES. PAGE.

CHAPTER V.

THE SPANISH MISSIONS.

CHAPTER VI.

ANTIQUITIES.

APPENDIX I.

APPENDIX II.

APPENDIX III.

THE FLORIDIAN PENINSULA.

CHAPTER I.

LITERARY HISTORY.

Introductory Remarks.—The Early Explorations.—The French Colonies.—The first Spanish Supremacy.—The English Supremacy.—The second Spanish Supremacy.—The Supremacy of the United States.—Maps and Charts.

In the study of special and local history, the inquirer finds his most laborious task is to learn how much his predecessors have achieved. It is principally to obviate this difficulty in so far as it relates to a very interesting, because first settled portion of our country, that I present the following treatise on the bibliographical history of East Florida. A few words are necessary to define its limits, and to explain the method chosen in collocating works.

In reference to the latter, the simple and natural plan of grouping into one section all works of whatever date, illustrating any one period, suggests itself as well adapted to the strongly marked history of Florida, however objectionable it might be in other cases. These periods are six in number, and consequently into six sections a bibliography naturally falls. The deeds of the early explorers, the settlement and subsequent destruction of the French, the two periods when Spain wielded the sovereign power, the intervening supremacy of England, and lastly, since it became attached to the United States, offer distinct fields of research, and are illustrated by different types of books. Such an arrangement differs not materially from a chronological adnumeration, and has many advantages of its own.

Greater difficulty has been experienced in fixing the proper limits of such an essay. East Florida itself has no defined boundaries. I have followed those laid down by the English in the Definitive Treaty of Peace of the 10th of February, 1763, when for the first time, East and West Florida were politically distinguished. The line of demarcation is here stated as "the Apalachicola or Chataouche river." The Spaniards afterwards included all that region lying east of the Rio Perdido. I am aware that the bibliography of the Spanish settlement is incomplete, unless the many documents relating to Pensacola are included, but at present, this is not attempted. It has been deemed advisable to embrace not only those works specially devoted to this region, but also all others containing original matter appertaining thereto. Essays and reviews are mentioned only when of unusual excellence; and a number of exclusively political pamphlets of recent date have been designedly omitted.

As I have been obliged to confine my researches to the libraries of this country, it will be readily understood that a complete list can hardly be expected. Yet I do not think that many others of importance exist in Europe, even in manuscript; or if so, they have escaped the scrutiny of the laborious Gustav Haenel, whose *Catalogi Librorum Manuscriptorum* I have examined with special reference to this subject. It is proper to add that the critical remarks are founded on personal examination in all cases, except where the contrary is specified.

§ 1.—The Early Explorations. 1512–1562.

No distinct account remains of the two voyages (1512, 1521,) of the first discoverer and namer of Florida, Juan Ponce de Leon. What few particulars we have concerning them are included in the general histories of Herrera, Gomara, Peter Martyr, and of lesser writers. However much the historian may regret this, it has had one advantage,—the romantic shadowing that hung over his aims and aspirations is undisturbed, and has given them as peculiar property to the poet and the novelist.

Of Pamphilo de Narvaez, on the contrary, a much inferior man, we have far more satisfactory relations. His Proclamation to the Indians[1] has been justly styled a curious monument of the spirit of the times. It was occasioned by a merciful (!) provision of the laws of the Indies forbidding war to be waged against the natives before they had been formally summoned to recognize the authority of the Pope and His Most Catholic Majesty. Should, however, the barbarians be so contumacious as to prefer their ancestral religion to that of their invaders, or their own chief to the Spanish king, then, says Narvaez, "With the aid of God and my own sword I shall march upon you; with all means and from all sides I shall war against you; I shall compel you to obey the Holy Church and his Majesty; I shall seize you, your wives and your

[1] Sommation à faire aux Habitants des Contrees et Provinces qui s'étendent depuis la Rivière des Palmes et le cap de la Floride. Extrait du livre des copies des Provinces de la Floride, Seville Chambre du Commerce, 1527. It is the first piece in Ternaux-Compans' *Recueil des Pièces sur la Floride.*

children; I shall enslave you, shall sell you, or otherwise dispose of you as His Majesty may see fit; your property shall I take, and destroy, and every possible harm shall I work you as refractory subjects." Thus did cruelty and avarice stalk abroad in the garb of religion, and an insatiable rapacity shield itself by the precepts of Christianity.

Among the officers appointed by the king to look after the royal interest in this expedition, holding the post of comptroller or factor (Tesorero), was a certain Alvar Nuñez, of the distinguished family of Cabeza de Vaca or the Cow's Head; deriving their origin and unsonorous name from Martin Alhaja, a mountaineer of Castro Ferral, who, placing the bones of a cow's head as a landmark, was instrumental in gaining for the Christians the decisive battle of Las Navas de Tolosa (1212), and was ennobled in consequence. When war, disease, and famine had reduced the force of Narvaez from three hundred to only half a dozen men, Alvar Nuñez was one of these, and after seven years wandering, replete with the wildest adventure, returned to Spain, there to receive the government of a fleet and the appointment of Adelantado to the unexplored regions around the Rio de la Plata. Years afterwards, when his rapacity and reckless tyranny had excited a mutiny among his soldiers and the animosity of his associates, or, as his defenders maintain, his success their envy and ill-will, he was arraigned before the council of the Indies in Spain. While the suit was pending, as a stroke of policy in order to exculpate his former life and set forth to the world his steadfast devotion to the interests of the king, in conjunction with his secretary Pedro Fernandez he wrote and published two works, one under his own supervision detailing his adventures in Florida,[1] the other his transactions in South America. Twenty-seven years had elapsed since the expedition of Narvaez, and probably of the few that escaped, he alone survived. When we consider this, and the end for which the book was written, what wonder that we find Alvar Nuñez always giving the best advice which Narvaez never follows, and always at hand though other men fail; nor, if we bear in mind the credulous spirit of the age and nation, is it marvellous that the astute statesman relates wondrous miracles, even to healing the sick and raising the dead, that he performed, proving that it was, as he himself says, "the visible hand of God" that protected him in his perilous roamings. Thus it happens that his work is "disfigured by bold exaggerations and the wildest fictions," tasking even Spanish credulity to such an extent that Barcia prefaced his edition of it with an *Examen Apologetico* by the erudite Marquis of Sorito, who, marshalling together all miraculous deeds recorded, proves conclusively that Alvar Nuñez tells the truth as certainly as many venerable abbots and fathers of the Church. However much this detracts from its trustworthiness, it is invaluable for its ethnographical data, and as the only extant history of the expedition, the greatest miracle of all still remaining, that half a dozen unprotected men, ignorant of the languages of the natives and of

[1] Naufragios de Alvar Nuñez Cabeza de Vaca en la Florida, Valladolid, 1555; republished by Barcia, in the Historiadores Primitivos de las Indias Occidentales, Tomo II., Madrid, 1749; translated by Ramusio, Viaggi, Tom. III., Venetia, 1556, from which Purchas made his abbreviated translation, Vol. IV., London, 1624; translated entire, with valuable notes and maps by Buckingham Smith, Washington, 1851. French translation by Ternaux-Compans, Paris, 1837.

their proper course, should have safely journeyed three thousand miles, from the bay of Apalache to Sonora in Mexico, through barbarous hordes continually engaged in internecine war. Of the many eventful lives that crowd the stormy opening of American history, I know of none more fraught with peril of every sort, none whose story is more absorbing, than that of Cabeza de Vaca.

The unfortunate termination of Narvaez's undertaking had settled nothing. Tales of the fabulous wealth of Florida still found credence in Spain; and it was reserved for Hernando de Soto to disprove them at the cost of his life and fortune. There are extant five original documents pertaining to his expedition.

First of these in point of time is his commission from the emperor Charles V.[1]

The next is a letter written by himself to the Municipality of Santiago,[2] dated July 9, 1539, describing his voyage and disembarkation. Besides its historical value, which is considerable as fixing definitely the time and manner of his landing, it has additional interest as the only known letter of De Soto; short as it is, it reveals much of the true character of the man. The hopes that glowed in his breast amid the glittering throng on the quay of San Lucar de Barrameda are as bright as ever: "Glory be to God," he exclaims,

[1] Asiento y capitulacion hecho por el capitan Hernando de Soto, con el Emperador Carlos V., para la Conquista y Poblacion de la Provincia de la Florida, y encomienda de la Gobernacion de la Isla de Cuba, 1537. Printed in 1844, in the preface to the Portuguese Gentleman's Narrative, by the Lisbon Academy of Sciences, from the manuscript in the Hydrographical Bureau of Madrid.

[2] Lettre écrite par l'Adelantade Soto, au Corps Municipal de la Ville de Santiago, de l'Isle de Cuba. In Ternaux-Compans' Recueil des Pieces sur la Floride.

"every thing occurs according to His will; He seems to take an especial care of our expedition, which lives in Him alone, and Him I thank a thousand times." The accounts from the interior were in the highest degree encouraging: "So many things do they tell me of its size and importance," he says, speaking of the village of Ocala, "that I dare not repeat them." Blissful ignorance of the old cavalier, over which coming misfortune cast no presageful shadow!

The position that Alvar Nuñez occupied under Narvaez was filled in this expedition by Luis Hernández de Biedma, and like Nuñez, he was lucky enough to be among the few survivors. In 1544, shortly after his return, he presented the king a brief account of his adventures.[1] He dwells on no particulars, succinctly and intelligibly mentions their course and the principal provinces through which they passed, and throws in occasional notices of the natives. The whole has an air of honest truth, differs but little from the gentleman of Elvas except in omission, and where there is disagreement, Biedma is often more probable.

When the enthusiasm for the expedition was at its height, and the flower of Spanish chivalry was hieing to the little port of San Lucar of Barrameda, many Portuguese of good estate sought to enroll themselves beneath its banners. Among these, eight hidalgos sallied forth from the warlike little town of Elvas (Evora) in the province of Alemtejo. Fourteen years after the disastrous close of the undertaking, one of

[1] Relation de ce que arriva pendant le Voyage du Capitaine Soto, et Details sur la Nature des pays qu'il parcourut, par Luis Hernandez de Biedma; first printed in Ternaux-Compan's *Recueil;* Eng. trans. by Rye, appended to the Hackluyt Society's edition of the Portuguese Gentleman's Narrative, London, 1852.

their number published anonymously in his native tongue the first printed account of it.[1] Now which it was will probably ever remain an enigma. Because Alvaro Fernandes is mentioned last, he has been supposed the author,[2] but unfortunately for this hypothesis, Alvaro was killed in Apalache.[3] So likewise we have notices of the deaths of Andres de Vasconcelo and Men Roiz Pereira (Men Rodriguez); it is not likely to have been Juan Cordes from the very brief account of the march of Juan de Añasco, whom this hidalgo accompanied; so it lies between Fernando and Estevan Pegado, Benedict Fernandez, and Antonio Martinez Segurado. I find very slight reasons for ascribing it to either of these in preference, though the least can be objected to the latter. Owing to this uncertainty, it is usually referred to as the Portuguese Gentleman's Narrative. Whoever he was, he has left us by all odds the best history of the expedition. Superior to Biedma in completeness, and to La Vega in accu-

[1] Relacão Verdadeira dos Trabalhos q̃ ho Gouernador dõ Fernãdo d' Souto y certos Fidalgos Portugueses passarom no d' scobrimẽto da provincia da Frolida. Agora nouamẽte feita per hũ Fidalgo Deluas, 8vo., Evora, 1557; reprinted, 8vo., Lisboa, 1844, by the Academia Real das Sciencias, with a valuable preface. It was "contracted" by Purchas, vol. IV., London, 1624; translated entire by Hackluyt, under the title, "Virginia richly valued by the Description of Florida, her next Neighbor," published both separately and in his Collections, vol. V., and subsequently by Peter Force, Washington, 1846, and by the Hackluyt Society, with a valuable introduction by J. T. Rye, London, 1852; another "very inferior" translation from the French, London, 1686. French trans. by M. D. C. (M. de Citri de la Guette), 12mo., Paris, 1685, and again in two parts, 1707–9. Dutch trans. in Van der Aa's Collection, 8vo., 1706, with "schoone kopere Platen," and a map.

[2] Buckingham Smith, Translation of Cabeza de Vaca, p. 126.

[3] Herrera, Dec. VII., cap. x., p. 16.

racy, of a tolerably finished style and seasoned with a dash of fancy, it well repays perusal even by the general reader.

The next work that comes under our notice is in some respects the most remarkable in Spanish Historical Literature. When the eminent critic and historian Prescott awarded to Antonio de Solis the honor of being the first Spanish writer who treated history as an art, not a science, and first appreciated the indissoluble bond that should ever connect it to poetry and belles-lettres, he certainly overlooked the prior claims of Garcias Laso or Garcilasso de la Vega. Born in Cusco in the year 1539,[1] claiming by his mother the regal blood of the Incas, and by his father that of the old Spanish nobility, he received a liberal education both in Peru and Spain. With a mind refined by retirement, an imagination attuned by a love of poetry and the drama, and with a vein of delicate humor, he was eminently qualified to enter into the spirit of an undertaking like De Soto's. His Conquest of Florida[2]

[1] Ticknor, in his History of Spanish Literature, says 1540; the Biographie Universelle, 1530; errors that may be corrected from the Inca's own words: "Yo nasci el año mil y quinientes y treinta y nueve." Commentarios Reales, Parte Segunda, Lib. II., cap. xxv.

[2] La Florida del Inca; Historia del Adelantado Hernando de Soto, Governador y Capitan General del Reino de la Florida, y de otros Heroicos Caballeros, Españoles y Indios; 4to, Lisbona, 1605; folio, Madrid, 1723; 12mo., Madrid, 1803. French trans. by St. Pierre Richelet, Paris, 1670, and 1709; Leyde, 1731; La Haye, 1735; by J. Badouin, Amsterdam, 1737. German trans. from the French, by H. S. Meier, Zelle, 1753; Nordhausen, 1785. Fray Pedro Abiles in the Censura to the second Spanish edition, speaks of a garbled Dutch translation or imitation, under the title (I retain his curious orthography), *Der West Indis che Spiegel Durch Athanasium Inga, Peruan von Cusco, T. Amsterdam, by Broer Jansen*, 1624.

is a true historical drama, whose catastrophe proves it a tragedy. He is said to lack the purity of Mariana, and not to equal De Solis in severely artistic arrangement; but in grace and fascination of style, in gorgeous and vivid picturing, and in originality of diction—for unlike his cotemporaries, La Vega modelled his ideas on no Procustean bed of classical authorship—he is superior to either. None can arise from the perusal of his work without agreeing with Southey, that it is "one of the most delightful in the Spanish language." But when we descend to the matter of facts and figures, and critically compare this with the other narratives, we find the Inca always gives the highest number, always makes the array more imposing, the battle more furious, the victory more glorious, and the defeat more disastrous than either. We meet with fair and gentle princesses, with noble Indian braves, with mighty deeds of prowess, and tales of peril, strange and rare. Yet he strenuously avers his own accuracy, gives with care his authorities, and vindicates their veracity. What then were these? First and most important were his conversations with a noble Spaniard who had accompanied De Soto as a volunteer. His name does not appear, but so thorough was his information and so unquestioned his character, that when the Council Royal of the Indies wished to inquire about the expedition, they summoned him in preference to all others. What he related verbally, the Inca wrote down, and gradually moulded into a narrative form. This was already completed when two written memoirs fell into his hands. Both were short, inelegant, and obscure, the productions of two private soldiers, Alonso de Carmona and Juan Coles, and only served to settle with more accuracy a few particulars. Though the narrative published at Elvas had been out nearly half a century before La Vega's work appeared, yet he had evidently never seen it; a piece of oversight less wonderful in the sixteenth century than in these index and catalogue days. They differ much, and although most historians prefer the less ambitious statements of the Portuguese, the Inca has not been left without defenders.

Chief among these, and very favorably known to American readers, is Theodore Irving.[1] When this writer was pursuing his studies at Madrid, he came across La Vega's Historia. Intensely interested by the facts, and the happy diction in which they were set forth, he undertook a free translation; but subsequently meeting with the other narratives, modified his plan somewhat, aiming to retain the beauties of the one, without ignoring the more moderate versions of the others. In the preface and appendix to his History of Florida, he defends the veracity of the Inca, and exhibits throughout an evident leaning toward his ampler estimates. His composition is eminently chaste and pleasing, and La Vega may be considered fortunate in having obtained so congenial an admirer. Entering fully into the spirit of the age, thoroughly versed in the Spanish character and language, and with such able command of his native tongue, it is to be regretted that the duties of his position have prevented Mr. Irving from further labors in that field for which he has shown himself so well qualified.

Many attempts have been made to trace De Soto's route. Those of Homans, Charlevoix, Guillaume de l'Isle and other early writers were foiled by their want

[1] The Conquest of Florida by Hernando de Soto, 2 vols. 8vo., Philadelphia, 1835; revised edition, 1 vol., 8vo., New York, 1851, with a map of De Soto's route.

of correct geographical knowledge.[1] Not till the present century was anything definite established. The naturalist Nuttall[2] who had personally examined the regions along and west of the Mississippi, and Williams[3] who had a similar topographical acquaintance with the peninsula of Florida, did much toward determining either extremity of his course, while the philological researches of Albert Gallatin on the Choktah confederacy[4] threw much light on the intermediate portion. Dr. McCulloh,[5] whose indefatigable labors in the field of American archæology deserve the highest praise, combined the labors of his predecessors and mapped out the march with much accuracy. Since the publication of his work, Dr. J. W. Monette,[6] Col. Albert J. Pickett,[7] Alexander Meek,[8] Theodore Irving,[9] Charles Guyarre,[10] L. A. Wilmer,[11] and others

[1] Charlevoix' scheme may be found in his Histoire de la Nouvelle France; De l'Isle's in the fifth volume of the Voyages au Nord, and in his Atlas Nouveau; Homans' is quoted by Warden in the Chronologie Historique de l'Amerique; all in the first half of the eighteenth century.

[2] Travels into the Arkansa Territory, in 1819, Phila., 1821.

[3] Natural and Civil History of Florida.

[4] Transactions of the American Antiquarian Society, vol. II.

[5] Antiquarian Researches.

[6] History of the Discovery and Settlement of the Valley of the Mississippi, New York, 1846, vol. I.

[7] History of Alabama, and incidentally of Georgia and Mississippi, vol. I.

[8] Southern Monthly Magazine and Review for Jan., 1839.

[9] History of the Conquest of Florida.

[10] History of Louisiana.

[11] Life, Travels, and Adventures of Ferdinand de Soto, 8vo., Philadelphia, 1858; an excellent popular compend.—Mr. Schoolcraft, in the third volume of the History of the Indian Tribes, has described from personal examination the country in the vicinity of the Ozark mountains, with reference to the westernmost portion of De Soto's route.

have bestowed more or less attention to the question. A very excellent resumé of most of their labors, with an accompanying map, is given by Rye in his introduction to the Hackluyt Society's edition of the Portuguese Gentleman's Narrative, who also adds a tabular comparison of the statements of this and La Vega's account.

From the failure of De Soto's expedition to the settlement of the French at the mouth of the St. John's, no very active measures were taken by the Spanish government in regard to Florida.

A vain attempt was made in 1549 by some zealous Dominicans to obtain a footing on the Gulf coast. A record of their voyage, written probably by Juan de Araña, captain of the vessel, is preserved;[1] it is a confused account, of little value.

The Compte-Rendu of Guido de las Bazares,[2] who explored Apalache Bay (Bahia de Miruelo) in 1559, to which is appended an epitome of the voyage of Angel de Villafañe to the coasts of South Carolina in 1561, and a letter from the viceroy of New Spain[3] relating to the voyage of Tristan de Arellano to Pensacola Bay (Santa Maria de Galve), are of value in verifying certain important dates in the geographical history of our country; and as they indicate, contrary

[1] Relation de la Floride pour l' Illustrissime Seigneur, Vice Roi de la Nouvelle Espagne, apporté par Frére Gregorio de Beteta; in Ternaux-Compans' *Recueil.*

[2] Compte Rendu par Guido de las Bazares, du voyage qu'il fait pour découvrir les ports et les baies qui sont sur la côte de la Floride; in Ternaux-Compans' *Recueil.*

[3] Lettre du vice-roi de la Nouvelle Espagne, Don Luis de Velasco, à sa Sacrée Majesté, Catholique et Royale, sur les affaires de la Floride. De Mexico, le 24 Septembre, 1559; in Ternaux-Compans' *Recueil.*

to the assertion of a distinguished living historian,[1] that the Spaniards had *not* wholly forgotten that land, "the avenues to which death seemed to guard."

Much more valuable than any of these is the memoir of Hernando D'Escalante Fontanedo.[2] This writer gives the following account of himself: born of Spanish parents in the town of Carthagena in 1538, at the age of thirteen he was sent to Spain to receive his education, but suffering shipwreck off the Florida coast, was spared and brought up among the natives, living with various tribes till his thirtieth year. He adds that in the same ship with him were Don Martin de Guzman, Hernando de Andino, deputy from Popayan, Alonso de Mesa, and Juan Otis de Zarate. Now at least one of these, the last mentioned, was never shipwrecked at any time on Florida, and in the very year of the alleged occurrence (1551) was appointed captain in a cavalry regiment in Peru, where he remained for a number of years;[3] nor do I know the slightest collateral authority for believing that either of the others suffered such a casuality. He asserts, moreover, that after his return to Spain he sought the post of interpreter under Aviles, then planning his attack on the Huguenots. But as this occurred in 1565, how could he have spent from his thirteenth to his thirtieth year, beginning with 1551, a prisoner among the Indians? In spite of these contradictions, there remains enough to make his memoir of great worth. He boasts that he could

[1] Bancroft, History of the United States, vol. I., p. 60.

[2] Memoire sur la Floride, ses Côtes et ses Habitants, qu' aucun de ceux qui l'ont visité ont su d'écrire; in Ternaux-Compans' *Recueil.*

[3] Herrera, Dec. VIII., lib. IX., cap. xviii.

speak four Indian tongues, that there were only two with which he was not familiar, and calls attention to what has since been termed their "polysynthetic" structure. Thus he mentions that the phrase *se-le-te-ga, go and see if any one is at the look-out,* is compounded partially of *tejihue, look-out;* "but in speaking," he observes, "the Floridians abridge their words more than we do." Though he did not obtain the post of interpreter, he accompanied the expedition of Aviles, and takes credit to himself for having preserved it from the traitorous designs of his successful rival: "If I and a mulatto," he says, "had not hindred him, all of us would have been killed. Pedro Menendez would not have died at Santander, but in Florida, where there is neither river nor bay unknown to me." For this service they received no reward, and he complains: "As for us, we have not received any pay, and have returned with broken health; we have gained very little therefore in going to Florida, where we received no advancement." Muñoz appended the following note to this memoir: "Excellent account, though of a man unaccustomed to writing, which is the cause of the numerous meaningless passages it contains." Ternaux-Compans adds: "Without finding, as Muñoz, this account excellent, I thought it best to insert it here as containing valuable notices of the geography of Florida. It is often unintelligible; and notwithstanding all the pains I have taken in the translation, I must beg the indulgence of the reader." The geographical notices are indeed valuable, particularly in locating the ancient Indian tribes. The style is crude and confused, but I find few passages so unintelligible as not to yield to a careful study and a comparison with cotemporary history. The memoir is addressed,

"Tres puissant Seigneur," and was probably intended to get its author a position. The date of writing is nowhere mentioned, but as it was not long after the death of Aviles (1574), we cannot be far wrong in laying it about 1580.

§ 2.—The French Colonies. 1562–1567.

Several distinct events characterize this period of Floridian history. The explorations and settlements of the French, their extirpation by the Spaniards and the founding of St. Augustine, the retaliation of De Gourgues ——, as they constitute separate subjects of investigation, so they may be assumed as nuclei around which to group extant documents. Compendiums of the whole by later writers form an additional class.

First in point of time is Jean Ribaut's report to Admiral Coligny. This was never printed in the original, but by some chance fell into the hands of an Englishman, who published it less than ten months after its writer's return.[1] "The style of this translation is awkward and crude, but the matter is valuable, embracing many particulars not to be found in any other account; and it possesses a peculiar interest as

[1] The whole and true Discoverye of Terra Florida, (Englished, The Flourishing Land) conteyning as well the wonderful straunge Natures and Manners of the People, with the merveylous Commodities and Treasures of the Country; as also the pleasant Portes and Havens and Wayes thereunto, never found out before the last year, 1562. Written in French, by Captain Ribauld, the fyrst that whollye discovered the same, and now newly set forthe in Englishe, the xxx. of May, 1563. Reprinted by Hackluyt, in his small black letter volume of 1583, but not in the folio collection.

being all that is known to have come from the pen of Ribault."[1]

René Laudonnière, Ribaut's companion and successor in command, a French gentleman of good education and of cultivated and easy composition, devotes the first of his three letters to this voyage. For the preservation of his writings we are indebted to the collector Basanier, whose volume of voyages will be noticed hereafter. The two narratives differ in no important particulars, and together convey a satisfactory amount of information.

The second letter of Laudonnière, this time chief in command, is the principal authority on the next expedition of the French to Florida. It is of great interest no less to the antiquarian than the historian, as the dealings of the colonists continually brought them in contact with the natives, and the position of Laudonnière gave him superior opportunities for studying their manners and customs. Many of his descriptions of their ceremonies are as minute and careful as could be desired, though while giving them he occasionally pauses to excuse himself for dealing with such trifles.

Besides this, there is a letter from a volunteer of Rouen to his father, without name or date.[2] Interior evidence, however, shows it was written during the summer of 1564, and sent home by the return vessels which left Florida on the 28th July of that

[1] Jared Sparks, Life of Jean Ribault, American Biography, vol. VII., p. 147.

[2] Coppie d'vne Lettre venant de la Floride, envoyée à Rouen, et depuis au Seigneur d'Eueron, ensemble le Plan et Portraict du Fort que les François y ont faict. Paris, 1565; reprint, without the "Plan et Portraict," in Ternaux-Compans' *Recueil*.

year. This was the earliest account of the French colony printed on the continent. Its contents relate to the incidents of the voyage, the manners of the "sauvages," and the building of the fort, with which last the troops were busied at the time of writing.

This and Ribaut's report made up the scanty knowledge of the colonies of Coligny to be found in Europe up to the ever memorable year 1565; memorable and infamous for the foulest crime wherewith fanaticism had yet stained the soil of the New World; memorable and glorious, for in that year the history of our civilization takes its birth with the first permanent settlement north of Mexico. Two nations and two religions came into conflict. Fortunately we are not without abundant statements on each side. Five eye-witnesses lived to tell the world the story of fiendish barbarity, or divine Nemesis, as they variously viewed it.

On the former side, the third and last letter of Laudonniére is a brief but interesting record. Simple, straightforward, it proves him a brave man and worthy Christian. He lays much blame on the useless delay of Ribaut, and attributes to it the loss of Florida.

Much more complete is the pleasing memoir of N. C. Challeux (Challus, Challusius.)[1] He tells us in his dedicatory epistle that he was a native of Dieppe, a carpenter by trade, and over sixty years of age at the time of the expedition. In another passage he

[1] Histoire Memorable du dernier Voyage aux Indes, Lieu appellée la Floride, fait par le capitaine Jean Ribaut et entrepris par comandement du Roi en l'an 1565, Lyons, 1566; another edition at Dieppe the same year, with the title "Discours de l'Histoire de la Floride," &c. Sparks says, "At least three editions were published the same year." Ternaux-Compans republished the Lyons edition in his *Recueil*, which differs somewhat from that of Dieppe.

remarks, "Old man as I am, and all grey."[1] He escaped with Laudonniére from Fort Caroline, and depicts the massacre and subsequent events with great truth and quaintness. He is somewhat of a poet, somewhat of a scholar, and not a little of a moralizer. At the beginning of the first edition are verses descriptive of his condition after his return, oppressed by poverty, bringing nought from his long rovings but "a beautiful white staff in his hand." "The volume closes with another effusion of his muse, expressing the joy he felt at again beholding his beloved city of Dieppe."[2] He is much given to diverging into prayers and pious reflections on the ups and downs of life, the value of contentment, and kindred subjects, seasoning his lucubrations with classical allusions.

When Laudonniére was making up the complement of his expedition he did not forget to include a cunning limner, so that the pencil might aid the pen in describing the marvels of the New World he was about to visit. This artist, a native of Dieppe, Jacques le Moyne de Morgues by name, escaped at the massacre by the Spanish, returned with Laudonniére, and with him left the ship when it touched the coast of England. Removing to London he there married, and supported himself by his profession. During the leisure hours of his after years he sketched from memory many scenes from his voyage, adding in his native language a brief description of each, aiding his recollection by the published narratives of Challeux

[1] "Pour vieillard que je suis et tout gris;" Sparks, mistaking the last word for *gros*, rather ludicrously translates this, "Old man as he was and very corpulent."—Life of Jean Ribault, p. 148.

[2] Sparks, ibid., p. 149.

and Laudonniére, duly acknowledging his indebtedness.[1] These paintings were familiar to Hackluyt, who gives it as one reason for translating the collection of Basanier, that the exploits of the French, "and diver other things of chiefest importance are lively drawn in colours at your no smal charges by the skillful painter James Morgues, sometime living in the Blackfryers in London."[2] When the enterprising engraver De Bry came to London in 1587, intent on collecting materials for his great work the *Peregrinationes*, he was much interested in these sketches, and at the death of the artist, which occurred about this time, obtained them from his widow with their accompanying manuscripts. They are forty-three in number, principally designed to illustrate the life and manners of the natives, and, with a map, make up the second part of De Bry's collection. Each one is accompanied by a brief, well-written explanation in Latin, and at the close a general narrative of the expedition; together, they form a valuable addition to our knowledge of the aboriginal tribes and the proceedings of the Huguenots on the Riviére Mai.

The Spanish accounts, though agreeing as regards the facts with those of their enemies, take a very different theoretical view. In them, Aviles is a model of Christian virtue and valor, somewhat stern now and then, it is true, but not more so than the Church permitted against such stiff necked heretics. The massacre of the Huguenots is excused with cogent reason-

[1] Brevis Narratio eorum quæ in Floridâ Americæ Provinciâ, Gallis acciderunt, secundâ in illam Navigatione, Duce Renato de Laudonniere Classis præfecto: Anno MDLXIIII., Francofurti ad Mœnum, 1591.

[2] Epistle Dedicatorie, Vol. III., p. 364.

ing; indeed, what need of any excuse for exterminating this nest of pestilent unbelievers? Could they be ignorant that they were breaking the laws of nations by settling on Spanish soil? The Council of the Indies argue the point and prove the infringement in a still extant document.[1] Did they imagine His Most Catholic Majesty would pass lightly by this taunt cast in the teeth of the devoutest nation of the world?

The best known witness on their side is Don Solis de Meras. His *Memorial de todas las Jornadas y Sucesos del Adelantado Pedro Menendez de Aviles,* has never been published separately, but all the pertinent portions are given by Barcia in the *Ensayo Cronologico para la Historia de la Florida,* with a scrupulous fidelity (sin abreviar su contexto, ni mudar su estilo). It was apparently written for Aviles, from the archives of whose family it was obtained by Barcia. It is an interesting and important document, the work of a man not unaccustomed to using the pen.

Better than it, however, and entering more fully into the spirit of the undertaking, is the memoir of Lopez de Mendoza Grajales,[2] chaplain to the expedition, and a most zealous hater of heretics. He does not aim at elegance of style, for he is diffuse and obscure, nor yet at a careful historical statement, for he esteems

[1] This seems to have escaped the notice of Mr. Sparks. It is in Ternaux-Compans' *Recueil des Pièces sur la Floride,* appended to the Compte-Rendu of Guido de las Bazares, without a distinct title.

[2] Memoire de l'heureux resultat et du bon Voyage que Dieu notre Seigneur a bien voulu accorder à la flotte qui partit de la Ville de Cadiz pour se rendre à la Côte et dans la Province de la Floride, et dont était général l'illustre Seigneur Pedro Menendez de Aviles; in Ternaux-Compans' *Recueil.*

lightly common facts, but he does strive to show how the special Providence of God watched over the enterprise, how divers wondrous miracles were at once proof and aid of the pious work, and how in sundry times and places God manifestly furthered the holy work of bloodshed. A useful portion of his memoir is that in which he describes the founding of St. Augustine, entering into the movements of the Spaniards with more detail than does the last-mentioned writer.

When the massacre of the 19th September, 1565, became known in Europe, "the French were wondrously exasperated at such cowardly treachery, such detestable cruelty."[1] Still more bitterly were they aroused when they learned the inexcusable butchery of Ribaut and his men. These had been wrecked on the Floridian shore, and with difficulty escaped the waves only to fall into the hands of more fell destroyers on land. When this was heard at their homes, their "widows, little orphan children, and their friends, relatives and connections," drew up and presented to Charles IXL., a petition,[2] generally known as the *Epistola*

[1] "Les François furent merveilleusement oultrez d'une si lasche trahison, et d'une si detestable cruaulté. La Reprinse de la Floride ; Ternaux-Compans' *Recueil*, p. 306.

[2] Une Requête au Roi, faite en forme de Complainte par les Femmes Veufues, petits Enfans Orphelins, et autres leurs Amies, Parents et Alliez, de ceux qui ont été cruellement envahis par les Espagnoles en la France Antharctiques dite la Floride, Mai 22, 1566 : it is printed "in one of the editions of Challeux *Discours*, and also at the end of Chauveton's French translation of Benzoni, Geneva, 1579. There are two Latin translations, one by Chauveton appended to his Brevis Historia, and also to the sixth part of De Bry ; the other by an unknown hand contained in the second part. These are free translations, but they accord in the essential points." Jared Sparks, Appendix to Life of Ribaut, American Biography, Vol. VII., pp. 153–4.

Supplicatoria, setting forth the facts of the case and demanding redress.

Though the weak and foolish monarch paid no marked attention to this, a man arose who must ever be classed among the heroes of history. This was Dominique de Gourgues, a high born Bourdelois, who, inspired with an unconquerable desire to wreak vengeance on the perpetrators of the bloody deed, sold his possessions, and by this and other means raised money sufficient to equip an expedition. His entire success is well known. Of its incidents, two, histories are extant, both by unknown hands, and both apparently written some time afterwards. It is even doubtful whether either writer was an eyewitness. Both, however, agree in all main facts.

The one first written and most complete lay a long time neglected in the Bibliotheque du Roi.[1] Within the present century it has been twice published from the original manuscript. It commences with the discovery of America by Columbus; is well composed by an appreciative hand, and has a pleasant vein of philosophical comment running throughout. The details of the voyage are given in a careful and very satisfactory manner.

The other is found in Basanier, under the title "Le Quatrièsme Voyage des François en la Floride, sous le capitaine Gourgues, en l'an 1567;" and, except the Introduction, is the only portion of his volume not written by Laudonniére. By some it is considered merely an epitome of the former, but after a careful

[1] La Reprinse de la Floride par le capitaine Gourgues; Revue Retrospective, seconde série, Tome II.; Ternaux-Compans' *Recueil*. The latter was not aware of the prior publication in the Revue.

comparison I am more inclined to believe it writen by Basanier himself, from the floating accounts of his day or from some unknown relator. This seems also the opinion of his late editor.

The manuscript mentioned by Charlevoix as existing in his day in the family of De Gourgues, was either a copy of one of these or else a third of which we have no further knowledge.

Other works may moulder in Spanish libraries on this part of our narrative. We know that Barcia had access to certain letters and papers (Cartas y Papeles) of Aviles himself, which have never been published, and possessed the original manuscripts of the learned historiographer Pedro Hernandez del Pulgar, among which was a *Historia de la Florida,* containing an account of the French colonies written for Charles II. But it is not probable that these would add any notable increment to our knowledge.

The Latin tract of Levinus Apollonius,[1] of extreme rarity, a copy of which I have never seen, is probably merely a translation of Challeux or Ribaut, as no other original account except the short letter sent to Rouen had been printed up to the date of its publication. This Apollonius, whose real name does not appear, was a German, born near Bruges, and died at the Canary Islands on his way to America. He is better known as the author of *De Peruviæ Inventione, Libri V., Antwerpiæ,* 1567,[2] a scarce work, not without merit. On the fly-leaf of the copy in the Yale College library is the following curious note:

[1] De Navigatione Gallorum in Terram Floridam, deque clade an. 1565 ab Hispanis acceptâ. Antwerpiæ, 1568, 8vo. Barcia erroneously adds a second edition of 1583.

[2] Rich (Bibliotheca Americana) incorrectly states 1565.

"Struvius in Bibl. Antiq. hunc librum laudibus affert; et inter raros adnumerant David Clement, Bibl. Curieuse, Tom. I.; pag; 403, Jo. Vogt, Catal; libror; rarior; pag; 40, Freytag in Analec; Literar; pag; 31."

Some hints of the life of Levinus may be found in his Epistola Nuncupatoria to this work, and there is a scanty article on him in the Biographie Universelle.

A work of somewhat similar title[1] was published in 1578 by Vignon at Geneva appended to Urbain Chauveton's (Urbanus Calveton's) Latin translation of Benzoni. It is hardly anything more than a translation of Challeux, whom indeed Chauveton professes to follow, with some details borrowed from André Thevet which the latter must have taken from the MSS. of Laudonniére. The first chapter and two paragraphs at the end are his own. In the former he says "he had been chiefly induced to add this short history to Benzoni's work, in consequence of the Spaniards at the time perpetrating more atrocious acts of cruelty in the Netherlands than they had ever committed upon the savages."

Items of interest are also found in the general histories of De Thou, (Thuanus,) a cotemporary, of L'Escarbot, of Charlevoix, and other writers.

In our own days, what the elegant pen of Theodore Irving has accomplished for the expedition of De Soto, has been done for the early settlements on the St.

[1] De Gallorum Expeditione in Floridam et clade ab Hispanis non minus iniusté quam immaniter ipsis illata, Anno MDLXV. Brevis Historia; Calveton, Novæ Novi Orbis Historiæ, Genevæ, 1578; De Bry, Peregrinationes, Pars VI.; French trans. in Chauveton's French trans. of Benzoni, 1579. For the notice of this work I am principally indebted to Sparks.

Johns by the talented author of the Life of Ribault.[1] He has no need of praise, whose unremitting industry and tireless endeavors to preserve the memory of their forefathers are so well known and justly esteemed by his countrymen as Jared Sparks. With what thoroughness and nice discrimination he prosecutes his researches can only be fully appreciated by him who has occasion to traverse the same ground. His work is one of those finished monographs that leave nothing to be desired either as respects style or facts in the field to which it is devoted—a field "the most remarkable in the early history of that part of America, now included in the United States and Canada, as well in regard to its objects as its incidents." Appended to the volume is an "Account of the Books relating to the Attempts of the French to found a Colony in Florida." The reader will have seen that this has been of service to me in preparing the analogous portion of this essay; and I have had the less hesitation in citing Mr. Sparks' opinions, from a feeling of entire confidence in his judgment.

Before closing these two periods of bibliographical history, the labors of the collectors Basanier and Ternaux Compans, to whom we owe so much, should not pass unnoticed. The former is the editor of the letters of Laudonniére, three in number, describing the voyage of Ribaut, the building of Fort Caroline, and its destruction by the Spaniards, to which he adds an introduction on the manners and customs of the Indians, also by Laudonniére, and an account of the

[1] Life of John Ribault, comprising an account of the first Attempts of the French to found a Colony in North America, Boston, 1845; in Vol. VII. of Sparks' American Biography.

voyage of De Gourgues.[1] In this he was assisted by Hackluyt, who speaks of him as "my learned friend M. Martine Basanier of Paris," and who translated and published his collection the year after its first appearance. Little is known of Basanier personally; mention is made by M. de Fétis in his Biographie des Musiciens of a certain Martin Basanier who lived about this time, and is probably identical. In the same year with his collection on Florida he published a translation of Antonio de Espejo's History of the Discovery of New Mexico. The dedication of the "Histoire Notable" is to the "Illustrious and Virtuous Sir Walter Raleigh." According to the custom of those days, it is introduced by Latin and French verses from the pens of J. Auratus (Jacques Doré?), Hackluyt, and Basanier himself. As a curious specimen of its kind I subjoin the anagram of the latter on Walter Raleigh:

"WALTER RALEGH.

La vertu l'ha à gré.

En *Walter* cognoissant *la vertu* s'estre enclose,
J'ay combiné *Ralegh*, pour y voir quelle chose
Pourroit à si beau nom convenir à mon gré;
J'ay trouvé que c'estoit; *la vertu l'ha à grè.*"

The first edition is rare, and American historians are

[1] L'Histoire Notable de la Floride située es Indes Occidentales; Contenant les troys Voyages faits en icelle par certains Capitaines et Pilotes François, descrits par le Capitaine Laudonniére, qui y a commandé l'espace d'un an troys moys; à laquelle a esté adjousté un quatriesme voyage par le Capitaine Gourgues. Mise en lumière par M. Basanier, Gentil-homme François Mathematicien. Paris, 1586, 8vo., 124 pp; reprinted Paris, 1853, with an *Avertissement.* Eng. trans. London, 4to, 1586, by R. H. (Richard Hackluyt,) who included it in his folio of 1600, reprinted in 1812.

under great obligations to the Parisian publishers for producing a second, and for preserving the original text with such care.

The labors of Ternaux Compans throughout the entire domain of early American history, his assiduity in collecting and translating manuscripts, and in republishing rare tracts, are too well known and generally appreciated to need special comment. Among his volumes there is one devoted to Florida, containing eleven scarce or inedited articles, all of which are of essential importance to the historian.[1] These have been separately considered previously, in connection with the points of history they illustrate.

§ 3.—The First Spanish Supremacy. 1567–1763.

After the final expulsion of the French, Spain held the ascendancy for nearly two hundred years. Her settlements extended to the south and west, the natives were generally tractable, and at one period the colony flourished; yet there is no more obscure portion of the history of the region now included in the United States. Except the Chronological Essay of Barcia, which extends over only a fraction of this period, the accounts are few in number, meagre in information, and in the majority of instances, quite inaccessible in this country.

The verbal depositions of Pedro Morales and Nicolas Bourguignon,[2] captives brought by Sir Francis Drake

[1] Voyages, Relations, et Memoires Originaux pour servir à l'Histoire de l'Amerique; seconde série; Recueil des Pieces sur la Floride, Paris, 1841.

[2] The Relation of Pedro Morales, a Spanyard which Sir Francis Drake brought from St. Augustines in Florida, where

to London, from his attack on St. Augustine, (1586,) are among the earliest notices we possess. They were written out by Richard Hackluyt, and inserted in his collection as an appendix to Drake's Voyage. Both are very brief, neither filling one of his folio pages; they speak of the Indian tribes in the vicinity, but in a confused and hardly intelligible manner. Nicolas Bourguignon was a Frenchman by birth, and had been a prisoner among the Spaniards for several years. He is the "Phipher," mentioned in Drake's account, who escaped from his guards and crossed over to the English, playing the while on his fife the march of the Prince of Orange, to show his nationality.

Towards the close of the century, several works were published in Spain, of which we know little but their titles. Thus, mention is made of a geographical description of the country (*Descripcion y Calidades de la Florida*) by Barrientes, Professor of the Latin language at the University of Salamanca, about 1580. It is probably nothing more than an extract from the *Cosmographia*, attributed by some to this writer. Also, about the same time, Augustin de Padilla Davila, a Dominican, and Bishop of St. Domingo, published an ecclesiastical history of the See of Mexico and the progress of the faith in Florida.[1] Very little, however, had been achieved that early in the peninsular and consequently his work would in this respect interest

he remayned sixe yeeres, touching the state of those partes, taken from his mouth by Richard Hackluyt, 1586.

The relation of Nicholas Bourgoignon, aliâs Holy, whom Sir Francis Drake brought from St. Augustine, also in Florida, where he had remayned sixe yeeres, in mine and Master Heriot's hearing. Voyages, Vol. III., pp. 432–33.

[1] Varia Historia de la Nueva España y la Florida; Madrid, 1596; Valladolid, 1634.

us but little. The reports of the proceedings of the Council of the Indies, doubtless contain more or less information in regard to Florida; Barcia refers especially to those published in 1596.[1]

Early in the next century there appeared an account of the Franciscan missionaries who had perished in their attempts to convert the savages of Florida.[2] The author, Geronimo de Ore, a native of Peru, and who had previously filled the post of Professor of Sacred Theology in Cusco, was, at the time of writing, commissary of Florida, and subsequently held a position in the Chilian Church, (deinde commissarius Floridæ, demum imperialis civitatis Chilensis regni antistes.)[3] He was a man of deep erudition, and wrote various other works "very learned and curious," (mui doctos y curiosos.[4])

Pursuing a chronological order, this brings us to the peculiarly interesting and valuable literature of the Floridian aboriginal tongues. Here, as in other parts of America, we owe their preservation mainly to the labors of missionaries.

As early as 1568, Padre Antonio Sedeño, who had been deputed to the province of Guale, now Amelia Island, between the mouths of the rivers St. Johns and St. Marys, drew up a grammar and catechism of the indigenous language.[5] It was probably a scion of the

[1] Cedulas y Provisiones Reales de las Indias; Varios Informes y Consultos de differentes Ministros sobre las Cosas de la Florida; 4to Madrid, 1596.

[2] Relacion de los Martires que ha avido en la Florida; 4to, (Madrid?) 1604.

[3] Nicolas Antonio, Bibliotheca Hispana Nova, Tom. II., p. 43, and Compare "Garcilasso, Commentarios Reales, Parte II., lib. VII."

[4] Barcia, Ensayo Cronologico, p. 181.

[5] "En breve tiempo hizó (Padre Antonio Sedeño) Arte para

Muskohge family, but as no philologist ever examined Sedeño's work—indeed, it is uncertain whether it was ever published—we are unprepared to speak decisively on this point.

The only works known to be in existence are those of Franceso de Pareja.[1] He was a native of the village of Auñon,[2] embraced the Franciscan theology, and was one of the twelve priests dispatched to Florida by the Royal Council of the Indies in 1592. He arrived there two years afterwards, devoted himself to converting the natives for a series of years, and about

aprenderla, y Catecismo para enseñar la Doctrina Cristiana à los Indios." Barcia, Ensayo Cronologico, p. 138. His labors have escaped the notice of Ludewig in his Literature of American Aboriginal Languages. Though they are the first labors, before him the French on the St. Lawrence had obtained lists of words in the native tongue which still remain, and Laudonniére, on the first voyage of Ribaut, (1562,) says of the Indians near the Savannah river, "cognoissans l'affection que j'avois de sçavoir leur langage, ils m' invitoient après à leur demander quelque chose. Tellement que mettant par escrit les termes et locutions indiennes, je pouvois entendre la plus grande part de leur discours. Hist. Notable de la Floride, p. 29. Unfortunately, however, he did not think these worthy of publication.

[1] Confessionario en Lengua Castellana y Timuquana. Impreso con licencia en Mexico, en la Emprenta de la viuda de Diego Lopez Daualos; Año de 1613, 12mo., 238 leaves. Nicolas Antonio says 1612, 8vo., but this is probably a mistake.

Grammatica de la Lengua Timuquana, 8vo., Mexico, 1614; not mentioned by Ludewig.

Catecismo y Examen para los que comulgan, 8vo., Mexico, 1614; reprinted "en la imprenta de Juan Ruyz," 8vo., 1627.

[2] Ludewig says Toledo; Torquemada calls him "Natural de Castro-Urdiales," but Nicolas Antonio says expressly, "Franciscus de Pareja, Auñonensis (Toletanæ dioecesis Auñon oppidum est)." Bibliotheca Hispana Nova, Tom. I., p. 456. Besides this writer, see for particulars of the life of Pareja, Torquemada, Monarquia Indiana, Lib. XIX., cap. xx., p. 350, and Barcia, Ensayo Cronologico, pp. 167, 195, 203.

1610 removed to the city of Mexico. Here he remained till the close of his life, in 1638, (January 25, O. S.,) occupied in writing, publishing, and revising a grammar of the Timuquana language, prevalent around and to the north of St. Augustine, and devotional books for the use of the missionaries. They are several in number, but all of the utmost scarcity. I cannot learn of a single copy in the libraries of the United States, and even in Europe; Adelung, with all his extensive resources for consulting philological works, was obliged to depend altogether on the extracts of Hervas, who, in turn, confesses that he never saw but one, and that a minor production of Pareja. This is the more to be regretted, as any one in the slightest degree acquainted with American philology must be aware of the absolute dearth of all linguistic knowledge concerning the tribes among whom he resided. His grammar, therefore, is second to none in importance, and no more deserving labor could be pointed out than that of rendering it available for the purposes of modern research by a new edition.

A *Doctrina Cristiana* and a treatise on the administration of the Sacraments are said to have been written in the Tinqua language of Florida by Fray Gregorio Morrilla, and published "the first at Madrid, 1631, and afterwards reprinted at Mexico, 1635, and the second at Mexico, 1635."[1] What nation this was, or where they resided is uncertain.

The manuscript dictionary and catechism of the Englishman Andrew Vito, "en Lengua de Mariland en la Florida," mentioned in Barcia's edition of Pinelo, and included by Ludewig among the works on the

[1] Ludewig, Literature of American Aboriginal Languages, p. 242.

Timuquana tongue, evidently belonged to a language far to the north of this, probably to one spoken by a branch of the Lenni Lennapes.

Throughout the seventeenth century notices of the colony are very rare. Travellers the most persistent never visited it. One only, Francesco (François) Coreal, a native of Carthagena in South America, who spent his life in wandering from place to place in the New World, seems to have recollected its existence. He was at St. Augustine in 1669, and devotes the second chapter of his travels to the province.[1] It derives its value more from the lack of other accounts than from its own intrinsic merit. His geographical notions are not very clear at best, and they are hopelessly confounded by the interpolations of his ignorant editor. The authenticity of his production has been questioned, and even his own existence disputed, but no reasonable doubts of either can be entertained after a careful examination of his work.

Various attempts were made by the Spanish to obtain a more certain knowledge of the shores and islands of the Gulf of Mexico during this period. A record of those that took place between 1685 and 1693[2] is mentioned by Barcia, but whether it was ever published or not, does not appear.

About this time the Franciscan Juan Ferro Macuardo occupied the post of inspector (Visitador General) of

[1] Voiages aux Indes Occidentales; traduits de l'Espagnol; Amsterdam, 1722. Dutch trans. the same year. Another edition under the title, Recueil de Voyages dans l'Amerique Meridionale, Paris, 1738, which Brunet does not notice.

[2] Relacion de los Viages que los Españoles han hecho ã las Costas del Seno Mexicano y la Florida desde el año de 1685 hasta el de 1693, con una nueva Descripcion de sus Costas.

the church in Florida under the direction of the bishop of Cuba. Apparently he found reason to be displeased with the conduct of certain of the clergy there, and with the general morality of the missions, and subsequently, in his memorial to the king,[1] handled without gloves these graceless members of the fraternity, telling truths unpleasant to a high degree. In consequence of these obnoxious passages, its sale was prohibited by the church on the ground that such revelations could result in no advantage.[2] Whether this command was carried out or not,—and it is said to have been evaded—the work is rare in the extreme, not being so much as mentioned by the most comprehensive bibliographers. Its value is doubtless considerable, as fixing the extent of the Spanish settlements, at this, about the most flourishing period of the colony. The *Respuesta* which it provoked from the pen of Francisco de Ayeta, is equally scarce.

The next book that comes under our notice we owe to the misfortune of a shipwreck. On the "twenty-third of the seventh month," 1696, a bark, bound from Jamaica to the flourishing colony of Philadelphia, was wrecked on the Floridian coast, near Santa Lucea, about 27° 8′, north latitude. The crew were treated cruelly by the natives and only saved their lives by pretending to be Spaniards. After various delays and much suffering they prevailed on their captors to conduct them to St. Augustine. Here Laureano de Torres, the governor, received them with much kind-

[1] Memorial en Derecho al Rei sobre la Visita à la Florida y otras Cosas, folio, Madrid, 1690.

[2] "Solo sirven de dar Escandalo al Vulgar en los Excesos impatados à unos y otros Individuos," Barcia, Ensayo Chronologico, p. 300.

ness, relieved their necessities, and furnished them with means to return home. Among the passengers was a certain Jonathan Dickinson a Quaker resident in Pennsylvania. On his arrival home, he published a narrative of his adventures,[1] that attracted sufficient attention to be reprinted in the mother country and translated into German. It is in the form of a diary, introduced by a preface of ten pages filled with moral reflections on the beneficence of God and His ready help in time of peril. The style is cramped and uncouth, but the many facts it contains regarding the customs of the natives and the condition of the settlement give it value in the eyes of the historian and antiquarian. Among bibliopolists the first edition is highly prized as one of the earliest books from the Philadelphia press. The printer, Reinier Jansen, was "an apprentice or young man" of William Bradford, who, in 1688, published a little sheet almanac, the first printed matter in the province.[2] After his return the author resided in Philadelphia till his death, in 1722, holding at one time the office of Chief Justice of Pennsylvania. He must not be confounded with his better known cotemporary of the

[1] God's Protecting Providence Man's Surest Help and Defence, In the times of the greatest difficulty and most Imminent danger, Evidenced in the Remarkable Deliverance of divers Persons from the devouring Waves of the Sea, amongst which they suffered Shipwrack, And also from the more cruelly devouring jawes of the inhumane Cannibals of Florida. Faithfully related by one of the Persons concerned therein. Philadelphia, 1699, 1701, and a *fourth* edition, 1751. London, 1700. German trans. Erstaunliche Geschichte des Schiffbruches den einige Personen im Meerbusen von Florida erlitten, Frankfort, 1784, and perhaps another edition at Leipzic.

[2] Thomas, History of Printing in America. vol. II. p. 25.

same name, staunch Presbyterian, and first president of the College of New Jersey, of much renown in the annals of his time for his fervent sermons and addresses.

The growing importance of the English colonies on the north, and the aggressive and irritable character of their settlers, gave rise at an early period of their existence to bitter feelings between them and their more southern neighbors, manifested by a series of attacks and reprisals on both sides, kept alive almost continually till the cession to England in 1763. So much did the Carolinians think themselves aggrieved, that as early as 1702, Colonel Moore, then governor of the province, made an impotent and ill-advised attempt to destroy St. Augustine; for which valorous undertaking his associates thought he deserved the fools-cap, rather than the laurel crown. An account of his Successes,[1] or more properly Misfortunes, published in England the same year, is of great rarity and has never come under my notice. Of his subsequent expedition, undertaken in the winter of 1703–4, for the purpose of wiping away the stigma incurred by his dastardly retreat, so-called, from St. Augustine, we have a partial account in a letter from his own pen to Sir Nathaniel Johnson, his successor in the gubernatorial post. It was published the next May in the Boston News, and has been reprinted by Carroll in his Historical Collections. The precise military force in Florida at this time may be

[1] The Successes of the English in America, by the March of Colonel Moore, Governor of South Carolina, and his taking the Spanish Town of St. Augustine near the Gulph of Florida. And by our English Fleete sayling up the River Darian, and marching to the Gold Mines of Santa Cruz de Cana, near Santa Maria. London, 1702; reprinted in an account of the South Sea Trade, London, 1711. *Bib. Primor. Amer.*

learned from the instructions given to Don Josef de Zuñiga, Governor-General in 1703, preserved by Barcia.

Some years afterwards Captain T. Nairns, an Englishman, accompanied a band of Yemassees on a slave hunting expedition to the peninsula. He kept a journal and took draughts on the road, both of which were in the possession of Herman Moll,[1] but they were probably never published, nor does this distinguished geographer mention them in any of his writings on his favorite science.

Governor Oglethorpe renewed these hostile demonstrations with vigor. His policy, exciting as it did much odium from one party and some discussion in the mother country, gave occasion to the publication of several pamphlets. Those that more particularly refer to his expedition against the Spanish, are three in number,[2] and, together with his own letters to his patrons, the Duke of Newcastle and Earl of Oxford,[3] and those of Captain McIntosh, leader of the Highlanders, and for some time a captive in Spain, which are still preserved in manuscript in the Library

[1] See the note on his New Map of the North Parts of America, London, 1720, headed "Explanation of an Expedition in Florida Neck by Thirty Three Iamasee Indians, Accompany'd by Capt. T. Nairn."

[2] A voyage to Georgia, begun in the year 1735, by Francis Moore; London, 1741; reprinted in the Collection of the Georgia Historical Society, Vol. I.

An Impartial Account of the Expedition against St. Augustine under the command of General Oglethorpe; 8vo., London, 1742. (*Rich.*)

Journal of an Expedition to the Gates of St. Augustine in Florida, conducted by General Oglethorpe. By G. L. Campbell; 8vo., London, 1744. (*Watts.*)

[3] They are in the Rev. George White's Historical Collections of Georgia, pp. 462, sqq., and in Harris's Memorials of Oglethorpe.

of the Georgia Historical Society,[1] furnish abundant information on the English side of the question; while the correspondence of Manuel de Montiano, Captain-General of Florida, extending over the years 1737–40, a part of which has been published by Captain Sprague[2] and Mr. Fairbanks,[3] but the greater portion still remaining inedited in the archives of St. Augustine, offers a full exposition of the views of their opponents.

A very important document bearing on the relations between the rival Spanish and English colonies, is the Report of the Committee appointed by the Commons House of Assembly of Carolina, to examine into the cause of the failure of Oglethorpe's expedition. In the Introduction[4] are given a minute description of the town, castle and military condition of St. Augustine, and a full exposition of the troubles between the two colonies, from the earliest settlement of the English upon the coast. Coming from the highest source, it deserves entire confidence.

Besides these original authorities, the biographies of Governor Oglethorpe, by W. B. O. Peabody, in Sparks' American Biography, by Thomas Spalding, in the publications of the Georgia Historical Society, and especially

[1] An extract may be found in Fairbank's History and Antiquities of St. Augustine.

[2] History of the Florida War. Ch. viii.

[3] History of St. Augustine. Ch. xiv.

[4] Statements made in the Introduction to a Report on General Oglethorpe's Expedition to St. Augustine. In B. R. Carroll's Hist. Colls. of South Carolina, Vol. II., New York, 1836. Various papers in the State Paper Office, London, mentioned in the valuable list in the first volume of the Colls. of the S. Car. Hist. Soc. (Charleston, 1857) which further illustrate this portion of Floridian history, I have, for obvious reasons, omitted to recapitulate here.

that by the Rev. T. M. Harris, are well worthy of comparison in this connection.

In the catalogue of those who have done signal service to American history by the careful collation of facts and publication of rare or inedited works, must ever be enrolled among the foremost Andres Gonzales Barcia. His three volumes of Historiadores Primitivos de las Indias Occidentales, are well known to every one at all versed in the founts of American history. His earliest work of any note, published many years before this, is entitled A Chronological Essay on the History of Florida.[1] He here signs himself, by an anagram on his real name, Don Gabriel de Cardenas z Cano, and is often referred to by this assumed title. In accordance with Spanish usage, under the term Florida, he embraced all that part of the continent north of Mexico, and consequently but a comparatively small portion is concerned with the history of the peninsula. What there is, however, renders it the most complete, and in many cases, the only source of information. The account of the French colonies is minute, but naturally quite one-sided. He is "in all points an apologist for his countrymen, and an implacable enemy to the Heretics, the unfortuuate Huguenots, who hoped to find an asylum from persecution in the forests of the New World."[2] The Essay is arranged in the form of annals, divided into decades and years, (Decadas, Años,) and extends from 1512 to 1723, inclusive. Neither this nor any of his writings can boast of elegance of style. In some portions he is even obscure, and at best is not readable by any but the professed historian.

[1] Ensayo Cronologico para la Historia General de la Florida, fol. Madrid, 1723.

[2] Jared Sparks, Life of Ribaut, p. 155.

Among writers in our own tongue, for indefatigability in inquiry, for assiduity in collecting facts and homeliness in presenting them, he may not inaptly be compared to John Strype, the persevering author of the Ecclesiastical Memorials.

His work was severely criticised at its appearance by Don Josef de Salazar, historiographer royal to Philip V, "a man of less depth of research and patient investigation than Barcia, but a more polished composer." He was evidently actuated in part by a jealousy of his rival's superior qualifications for his own post. The criticism repays perusal. None of Salazar's works are of any standing, and like many another, he lives in history only by his abuse of a more capable man.

In the preface to his History of Florida, Mr. Williams informs us that he had in his possession "a rare and ancient manuscript in the Spanish language, in which the early history of Florida was condensed, with a regular succession of dates and events." He adds, that the information here contained about the Catholic missions and the extent of the Spanish power had been "invaluable" to him. If this was an authentic manuscript, it probably dated from this period. Williams obtained it from Mr. Fria, an alderman of New York, and not understanding the language himself, had it translated. It is to be regretted that he has not imparted more of the "invaluable information" to his readers. The only passages which he quotes directly, induce me to believe that he was imposed upon by a forgery, or, if genuine, that the account was quite untrustworthy. Thus it spoke of a successful expedition for pearls to Lake Myaco, or Okee-chobee, which I need hardly say, is a body of fresh water, where the *Mya margaratifera* could not live. The extent of the

Franciscan missions is grossly exaggerated, as I shall subsequently show. Rome at no time chartered a great religious province in Florida, whose principal house was at St. Augustine;[1] nor does Mr. Williams' work exhibit any notable influx of previously unknown facts about the native tribes, though he says on this point, his manuscript was especially copious. On the whole, we need not bewail the loss, or lament the non-publication of this record.

The latest account of the Spanish colony during this period, is that by Captain Robinson, who visited the country in 1754. It is only a short letter, and is found appended to Roberts' History of Florida.

In the language of the early geographers, however, this name had a far more extensive signification, and many books bear it on their title pages which have nothing to do with the peninsula. Thus an interesting tract in Peter Force's collection entitled "A Relation of a Discovery lately made on the Coast of Florida," is taken up altogether with the shores of South Carolina. The superficial and trifling book of Daniel Coxe, insignificant in everything but its title, proposes to describe the Province "by the Spaniards called Florida," whereas the region now bearing this name, was the only portion of the country east of the Mississippi and south of the St. Lawrence *not* included in the extensive claim the work was written to defend. In the same category is Catesby's Natural History of Carolina, Florida, and the Bahama Islands. This distinguished naturalist during his second voyage to America, (1722) spent three years in Carolina, "and in the adjacent parts, which the Spaniards call Florida,

[1] Nat. and Civil Hist. of Fla., p. 175.

particularly that province lately honored with the name of Georgia." How much time he spent in the peninsula, or whether he was there at all, does not appear.

§ 4.—The English Supremacy. 1763–1780.

No sooner had England obtained possession of her new colony than a lively curiosity was evinced respecting its capabilities and prospects. To satisfy this, William Roberts, a professional writer, and author of several other works, compiled a natural and civil history of the country, which was published the year of the cession, under the supervision of Thomas Jefferys, geographer royal.[1] It ran through several editions, and though it has received much more praise than is its proper due, it certainly is a useful summary of the then extant knowledge of Florida, and contains some facts concerning the Indians not found in prior works. The natural history of the country is mentioned nowhere out of the title page; the only persons who paid any attention worth speaking of to this were the Bartrams, father and son. Their works come next under our notice.

John Bartram was born of a Quaker family in Chester county, Pennsylvania, in 1701. From his earliest youth he manifested that absorbing love for the natural sciences, especially botany, that in after years won for him from no less an authority than the immortal Linnæus, the praise of being "the greatest botanist

[1] An Account of the First Discovery and Natural History of Florida, with a Particular Detail of the several Expeditions made on that Coast. Collected from the best Authorities by William Roberts. Together with a Geographical Description of that Country, by Thomas Jefferys. 4to, London, 1763, pp. 102.

in the New World." He was also the first in point of time. Previously all investigations had been prosecuted by foreigners in a vague and local manner. Bartram went far deeper than this. On the pleasant banks of the Schuylkill, near Philadelphia, he constructed the first botanic garden that ever graced the soil of the New World; here to collect the native flora, he esteemed no journey too long or too dangerous. After the cession, he was appointed "Botanist to His Majesty for both the Floridas," and though already numbering over three-score years, he hastened to visit that land whose name boded so well for his beloved science. Accompanied only by his equally enthusiastic son William, he ascended the St. Johns in an open boat as far as Lake George, daily noting down the curiosities of the vegetable kingdom, and most of the time keeping a thermometrical record. On his return, he sent his journal to his friends in England under whose supervision, though contrary to his own desire, it was published.[1] It makes a thin quarto, divided into two parts paged separately. The first is a general description of the country, apparently a reprint of an essay by the editor, Dr. Stork, a botanist likewise, and member of the Royal Society, who had visited Florida. The second part is Bartram's diary, enriched with elaborate botanical notes and an Introduction by the editor. It is merely the daily jottings

[1] A description of East Florida. A Journal upon a Journey from St. Augustine up the River St. Johns as far as the Lakes. 4to., London, 1766; 1769; and a third edition whose date I do not know. Numerous letters interchanged between John Bartram and Peter Collinson relative to this botanical examination of Florida, embracing some facts not found in his Journal, are preserved in the very interesting and valuable Memorials of John Bartram and Humphrey Marshall, by Dr. Wm. Darlington, p. 268, sqq. (8vo. Phila., 1849.)

of a traveller and could never have been revised; but the matter is valuable both to the naturalist and antiquary.

The younger Bartram could never efface from his memory the quiet beauty and boundless floral wealth of the far south. About ten years afterwards therefore, when Dr. Fothergill and other patrons had furnished him the means to prosecute botanical researches throughout the Southern States, he extended his journey to Florida. He made three trips in the peninsula, one up the St. Johns as far as Long Lake, a second from "the lower trading house," where Palatka now stands, across the savannas of Alachua to the Suwannee, and another up the St. Johns, this time ascending no further than Lake George. The work he left is in many respects remarkable;[1] "it is written" said Coleridge "in the spirit of the old travellers." A genuine love of nature pervades it, a deep religious feeling breathes through it, and an artless and impassioned eloquence graces his descriptions of natural scenery, rendering them eminently vivid and happy. With all these beauties, he is often turgid and verbose, his transitions from the sublime to the common-place jar on a cultivated ear, and he is too apt to scorn anything less than a superlative. Hence his representations are exaggerated, and though they may hold true to him who sees unutterable beauties in the humblest flower, to the majority they seem the extravaganzas of fancy. He is generally reliable, however, in regard

[1] Travels through North and South Carolina, Georgia, East and West Florida, and the Cherokee Country, Phila., 1791; 1794. London, 1792 Dublin, 1793. French trans. by P. V. Benoist, Voyage dans les Parties Sud de l'Amerique, Septentrionale, Paris, 1801; 1807.

to single facts, and as he was a quick and keen observer of every remarkable object about him, his work takes a most important position among our authorities, and from the amount of information it conveys respecting the aborigines, is indispensable to the library of every Indianologist.

A very interesting natural history of the country is that written by Bernard Romans.[1] This author, in his capacity of engineer in the British service, lived a number of years in the territory, traversing it in various directions, observing and noting with care both its natural features and the manners and customs of the native tribes. On the latter he is quite copious and is one of our standard authors. His style is discursive and original though occasionally bombastic, and many of his opinions are peculiar and bold. Extensive quotations from him are inserted by the American translator in the Appendix to Volney's View of the United States. He wrote various other works, bearing principally on the war of independence. A point of interest to the bookworm in his History is that the personal pronoun I, is printed throughout as a small letter.

A work on a contested land title, privately printed in London for the parties interested about the middle of this period,[2] might possess some little interest from the accompanying plan, but in other respects is probably valueless. There is a manuscript work by John

[1] A Concise Natural History of East and West Florida. New York printed: sold by R. Aitken, Bookseller, opposite the London Coffee-House, Front Street, 1776.

[2] The case of Mr. John Gordon with respect to the Title to certain Lands in East Florida, &c. With an Appendix and Plan. 4to, pp. 76, London, 1772. (*Rich.*)

Gerard Williams de Brahm, preserved in the library of Harvard College, which "contains some particulars of interest relative to Florida at the period of the English occupation."[1] Extracts from it are given by Mr. Fairbanks, descriptive of the condition of St. Augustine from 1763 to 1771, and of the English in the province. This De Brahm was a government surveyor, and spent a number of years on the eastern coasts of the United States while a British province.

Among the many schemes set in motion for peopling the colony, that of Lord Rolls who proposed to transport to the banks of the St. Johns the *cypriennes* and degraded *femmes du pave* of London,[2] and that of Dr. Turnbull, are especially worthy of comment. The latter collected a colony from various parts of the Levant,—from Greece, from Southern Italy, and from the Minorcan Archipelago—and established his head quarters at New Smyrna. The heartless cruelty with which he treated these poor people, their birth-place and their fate, as well as the fact that from them most of the present inhabitants of St. Augustine receive their language, their character, and the general name of Minorcans, have from time to time attracted attention to their history. Besides notices in general works on Florida, Major Amos Stoddard in a work on Louisiana[3] sketches the colony's rise and progress, but he is an inaccurate historian and impeachable authority. It

[1] Fairbanks, Hist. and Antiqs. of St. Augustine, p. 164, seq.

[2] He did not meet with that success which attended a similar experiment in Canada, so amusingly described by Baron de La Hontan. For some particulars of interest consult Bartram, Travels, p. 94, seq., Vignoles, Obs. on the Floridas, p. 73.

[3] Sketches, Historical and Descriptive, of Louisiana, vol. I, 8vo, Ch. II. Philadelphia, 1812.

is the only portion of his chapter on the Floridas of any value. In 1827, an article upon them was published in France by Mr. Mease,[1] which I have not consulted, and a specimen of their dialect, the Mahonese, as it existed in 1843, in the *Fromajardis* or Easter Song, has been preserved by Bryant, and is a curious relic.[2]

§ 5.—The Second Spanish Supremacy. 1780–1821.

During this period few books were published on Florida and none whatever in the land of the regainers of the territory. The first traveller who has left an account of his visit thither is Johann David Schöpf,[3] a German physician who had come to America in 1777, attached to one of the Hessian regiments in the British service. At the close of the war he spent two years (1783–4) in travelling over the United States previous to returning home, a few weeks of which, in March, 1784, he passed in St. Augustine. He did not penetrate inland, and his observations are confined to a description of the town, its harbor and inhabitants,

[1] Notice sur le Colonie Greque établie à New Smyrna (Floride) dans l'année, 1768. Societe de Geographie, T. VII., p. 31. (*Koner.*)

[2] G. R. Fairbanks, Hist. and Antiqs. of St. Augustine, Ch. XVIII. See also for other particulars, Bartram, Travels, p. 144, and note, Vignoles, Obs. on the Floridas, p. 72, J. D. Schöpf, Reise---nach, Ost-Florida, B. II., s. 363, 367, seq., who knew Turnbull personally and defends him.

[3] Reise durch einige der mitlern und südlichen Vereinigten Nordamerikanischen Staaten nach Ost-Florida und der Bahama-Inseln. 2 Th., 8vo., Erlangen, 1788.

and some notices of the botany of the vicinity—for it was to natural history and especially medical botany that Schöpf devoted most of his attention during his travels. The difficulties of Spain with the United States in regard to boundaries gave occasion for some publications in the latter country. As early as 1797, the President addressed a message to Congress "relative to the proceedings of the Commissioner for running the Boundary Line between the United States and East and West Florida," which contains a resumé of what had been done up to that date.

Andrew Ellicott, Commissioner in behalf of the United States, was employed five years in determining these and other boundaries between the possessions of our government and those of His Catholic Majesty. He published the results partially in the Transactions of the American Philosophical Society, and more fully several years afterwards in a separate volume.[1] They are merely the hasty notes of a surveyor, thrown together in the form of a diary, without attempt at digestion or connection; but he was an acute and careful observer, and his *renseignements* on the topography of East Florida are well worth consulting. Among the notable passages is a vivid description of the remarkable meteoric shower of November 12, 1799, which he encountered off the south-western coast of Florida, and from which, conjoined with the observations of Humboldt at Cumana, and others, the periodicity of this phænomenon was determined by Palmer, of New Haven.

[1] The Journal of an Expedition during the years 1796–1800, for determining the Boundaries between the United States and the Possessions of his Catholic Majesty in America, 4to., Philadelphia, 1814.

A geographical account of Florida is said to have appeared at Philadelphia about this time, from the pen of John Mellish,[1] but unless it forms merely a part of the general geography of that author, I have been able to find nothing of the kind in the libraries of that city.

The article on Florida in the important work on America of Antonio de Alcedo,[2] derives some importance from the list of Spanish governors it contains, which, however, is not very perfect; but otherwise is of little service.

Serious difficulties between the Seminole Indians[3] and the whites of Georgia, occurred at an early date in this period arising from attempts of the latter to recapture fugitive slaves. These finally resulted in the first Seminole war, and attracted the attention of the general government. The action taken in respect to it may be found in the Ex. Doc. No. 119, 2d Session, XVth Congress, which contains "the official correspondence between the War Department and General Jackson; also that between General Jackson and General Gaines, together with the orders of each, as well as the correspondence between the Secretary of the Navy and Commodore Patterson, and the orders of the latter officer to Sailing-Master Loomis, and the final report of Sailing-Master Loomis and General Clinch;"[4] also in two messages of the President

[1] A Description of East and West Florida and the Bahama Islands, 1 Vol. 8vo. Philadelphia, 1813. (*Bib. Univ. des Voyages.*)

[2] Geographical and Historical Dictionary of America and the West Indies; translated, with valuable additions, by G. R. Thompson, 5 vols., 4to, London, 1812.

[3] An account of this tribe by Major C. Swan, who visited them in 1791, has been published by Schoolcraft in the fifth volume of the Hist. and Statistics of the Indian Tribes.

[4] Giddings, Exiles of Florida, p. 39, note.

during 1818, on the Seminole war, one of which contains the documents relative to Arbuthnot and Ambruster, the Cherokees, Chocktaws, &c., and in the speeches of the Hon. Robert Poindexter, and others. Dr. Monette and Mr. Giddings, in their historical works, have also examined this subject at some length.

Two accounts of the fillibustering expeditions that resulted in the forcible possession of Amelia Island by Captain MacGregor, have been preserved; one, "the better of the two," by an anonymous writer.[1] They are both rare, and neither have come under my inspection.

An important addition to our knowledge of East Florida during this period, is contained in the entertaining Letters of Dr. William Baldwin.[2] This gentleman, a surgeon in the United States Navy, and a devoted lover of botany, compelled to seek safety from a pulmonary complaint by taking refuge in a warm climate during the winter months, passed portions of several years, commencing with 1811, in East Florida and on the confines of Georgia, occupying himself in studying the floral wealth of those regions. He recorded his observations in a series of letters to Dr. Muhlenberg of Lancaster, and to the subsequent editor of his Remains, Dr. William Darlington, of West Chester, Pa., well known from his works on the local

[1] Narrative of a Voyage to the Spanish Main by the ship Two Friends, the Occupation of Amelia Island by McGregor, Sketches of the Province of East Florida, and Anecdotes of the Manners of the Seminole Indians, 8vo., London, 1819.

Memoir of Gregor McGregor, comprising - - - - a Narrative of the Expedition to Amelia Island. By M. Rafter. 8vo., Stockdale, 1820. (*Rich.*)

[2] Reliquiæ Baldwinianæ; Selections from the Correspondence of the late Wm. Baldwin, M. D., compiled by Wm. Darlington, M. D. 12mo. Phila., 1843.

and historical botany of our country, and whom I have already had occasion to advert to as the editor of the elder Bartram's Correspondence. While those to the former have no interest but to the professed botanist, his letters to the latter are not less rich in information regarding the condition of the country and its inhabitants, than they are entertaining from the agreeable epistolary style in which they are composed, and the thanks of the historian as well as the naturalist are due to their editor for rescuing them from oblivion. It was the expectation of Dr. Baldwin to give these observations a connected form and publish them under the subjoined title,[1] but the duties of his position and his untimely death prevented him from accomplishing this design. As far as completed, comprising eight letters, twenty pages in all, this work is appended to the Reliquiæ.

The cession of Florida to the United States, naturally excited considerable attention, both in England and our own country, manifested by the appearance of several pamphlets, the titles of two of the most noteworthy of which are given below.[2]

[1] Notices of East Florida, and the Sea Coast of the State of Georgia; in a series of Letters to a Friend in Pennsylvania. With an Appendix, containing a Register of the Weather, and a Calendarium Floræ. The friend here referred to was Dr. Wm. Darlington. The materials for the Calendarium are preserved in the letters to Dr. Muhlenberg.

[2] J. L. Rattenbury. Remarks on the Cession of Florida to the United States of America, and on the necessity of acquiring the Island of Cuba by Great Britain. Second edition, with considerable additions, printed exclusively in the Pamphleteer. London, 1819.

Memoir upon the Negotiations between Spain and the United States, which led to the Treaty of 1819; with a Statistical Notice of Florida, 8vo., Washington, 1821.

Numerous manuscripts pertaining to the history of the colony are said to have been carried away by the Catholic clergy at the time of the cession, many of which were deposited in the convents of Havana, and probably might still be recovered.

§ 6.—The Supremacy of the United States. 1821–1858.

No sooner had the United States obtained possession of this important addition to her territory, than emigrants, both from the old countries and from the more northern States, prepared to flock thither to test its yet untried capabilities. Information concerning it was eagerly demanded and readily supplied. In the very year of the cession appeared two volumes, each having for its object the elucidation of its geography and topography, its history, natural and civil.

One of these we owe to William Darby,[1] an engineer of Maryland, not unknown in our literary annals as a general geographer. It is but a compilation, hastily constructed from a mass of previously known facts, to satisfy the ephemeral curiosity of a hungry public. As far as is known of his life, the author never so much as set foot in the country whose natural history he proposes to give, and he will err widely who hopes to find in it that which the pretentious title-page bids him expect.

A much superior work is that of James Grant Forbes.[2] This gentleman was a resident of the ter-

[1] A Memoir of the Geography, and Natural and Civil History of East Florida, 8vo., Philadelphia, 1821.

[2] Sketches of the History and Topography of Florida, 8vo., New York, 1821.

ritory, and had ample opportunities for acquiring a pretty thorough knowledge of its later history, both from personal experience and from unpublished documents. He is consequently good authority for facts occurring during the British and later Spanish administrations. Though at the time of publication the subject of considerable praise, his work has since been denounced, though with great injustice, as "a wretched compilation from old works."[1]

The next year a little book appeared anonymously at Charleston.[2] The writer, apparently a physician, had travelled through Alachua county, and ascended the St. Johns as far as Volusia. It consists of a general description of the country, a diary of the journey through Alachua, and an account of the Seminole Indians with a vocabulary of their language. Some of his observations are not without value.

The next work in chronological order was written by Charles Vignoles, a "civil and topographical engineer," and subsequently public translator at St. Augustine. In the Introduction he remarks, "The following observations on the Floridas have been collected during a residence in the country; in which period several extensive journeys were made with a view of obtaining materials for the construction of a new map, and for the purpose now brought forward." He notices the history, topography, and agriculture, the climate and soil of the territory, gives a sketch of the Keys, some account of the Indians, and is quite full on

[1] Compare the North Am. Review, Vol. XIII., p. 98, with the same journal, Vol. XXVI., p. 482. (*Rich.*)

[2] Notices of East Florida, with an Account of the Seminole Nation of Indians. By a recent Traveller in the Province. Printed for the Author. 8vo. Charleston, 1822. pp. 105.

Land Titles, then a very important topic, and adds to the whole a useful Appendix of Documents relative to the Cession.[1] Vignoles is a dry and uninteresting composer, with no skill in writing, and his observations were rather intended as a commentary on his map than as an independent work.

Energetic attempts were shortly made to induce immigration. Hopes were entertained that a colony of industrious Swiss might be persuaded to settle near Tallahassie, where it was supposed silk culture and vine growing could be successfully prosecuted. When General Lafayette visited this country he brought with him a series of inquiries, propounded by an intelligent citizen of Berne, relative to the capabilities and prospects of the land. They were handed over to Mr. McComb of that vicinity. His answers[2] are tinged by a warm fancy, and would lead us to believe that in middle Florida had at last been found the veritable Arcadia. Though for their purpose well suited enough, for positive statistics it would be preferable to seek in other quarters.

In 1826, there was an Institute of Agriculture, Antiquities, and Science organized at Tallahassie. At the first (and, as far as I am aware, also the last) public meeting of this comprehensive society, Colonel Gadsden was appointed to deliver the opening address.[3]

[1] Observations on the Floridas. 8vo. New York, 1823. pp. 197.

[2] Answers of David B. McComb, Esq., with an accompanying Letter of General Lafayette. 8vo. Tallahassie, 1827. See the North Am. Review, Vol. XXVI., p. 478.

[3] Oration delivered by Colonel James Gadsden to the Florida Institute of Agriculture, Antiquities and Science, at its first Public Anniversary, Thursday, Jan. 4th, 1827. See the North Am. Review, Vol. XXV., p. 219.

This was afterwards printed and favorably noticed by some of the leading journals. Apparently, however, it contained little at all interesting either to the antiquarian or scientific man, but was principally taken up with showing the prospect of a rapid agricultural developement throughout the country.

Neither were general internal improvements slighted. A project was set on foot to avoid the dangerous navigation round the Florida Keys by direct transportation across the neck of the peninsula—a design that has ever been the darling hobby of ambitious Floridians since they became members of our confederacy, and which at length seems destined to be fulfilled. Now railroads, in that day canals were to be the means. As early as 1828, General Bernard, who had been dispatched for the purpose, had completed two levellings for canal routes, had sketched an accurate map on an extended scale, and had laid before the general government a report embracing a topographical and hydrographical description of the territory, the result of his surveys, with remarks on the inland navigation of the coast from Tampa to the head of the delta of the Mississippi, and the possible and actual improvements therein.[1] Notwithstanding these magnificent preparations, it is unnecessary to add, the canal is still unborn.

One great drawback to the progress of the territory was the uncertainty of Land Titles. During the Span-

[1] Message of the President in relation to the Survey of a Route for a Canal between the Gulf of Mexico and the Atlantic Ocean; with the Report of the Board of Internal Improvement on the same, with a general map annexed, February 28, 1829. A flowery article of ten pages may be found on this in the Southern Review, Vol. VI., p. 410.

ish administration nearly the whole had been parcelled out and conferred in grants by the king. Old claims, dating back to the British regime, added to the confusion. Many of both had been sold and resold to both Spanish and American citizens. In the Appendix to Vignoles, and in Williams' View of West Florida, many pages are devoted to this weighty and very intricate subject. Some of these claims were of enormous extent. Such was that of Mr. Hackley, which embraced the whole Gulf coast of the peninsula and reached many miles inland. This tract had been a grant of His Catholic Majesty to the Duke of Alagon, and it was an express stipulation on the part of the United States, acceded to by the king, that it should be annulled. But meanwhile the Duke had sold out to Mr. Hackley and others, who claimed that the king could not legally dispossess American citizens. A pamphlet was published[1] containing all the documents relating to the question, and the elaborate opinions of several leading lawyers, all but one in favor of Mr. Hackley. After a protracted suit, the Gordian knot was finally severed by an *ex post facto* decree of His Majesty, that a crown grant to a subject was in any case inalienable, least of all to a foreigner.

The work of Col. John Lee Williams just mentioned,[2] though ostensibly devoted to West Florida

[1] Titles and Legal Opinions on Lands in East Florida belonging to Richard S. Hackley, 8vo., Fayetteville, (N. Car.,) 1826, pp. 71. See the North American Review, Vol. XXIII., p. 432. Hackley's grant is laid down on Williams' Map.

[2] A View of West Florida, embracing its Topography, Geography, &c., with an Appendix treating of its Antiquities, Land Titles, and Canals, and containing a Chart of the Coast, a Plan of Pensacola, and the Entrance of the Harbor. 8vo. Phila., 1827, pp. 178.

takes a wider sweep than the title page denotes. Its author went to Florida in 1820, and was one of the commissioners appointed to locate the seat of government. While busied with this, he was struck with the marked deficiency of all the then published maps of the country, "and for my own satisfaction," he adds, "I made a minute survey of the coast from St. Andrew's Bay to the Suwannee, as well as the interior of the country in which Tallahassie is situated." A letter from Judge Brackenridge, alcalde of St. Augustine, principally consisting of quotations from Roberts, is all that touches on antiquities. Except this, and some accounts of the early operations of the Americans in obtaining possession, and the statements concerning Land Titles, the book is taken up with discussions of proposed internal improvements of very local and ephemeral interest.

All the details of any value that it contains he subsequently incorporated in his Civil and Natural History of the Territory, published ten years later. Most of the intervening time he spent in arduous personal researches; to quote his own words, "I have traversed the country in various directions, and have coasted the whole peninsula from Pensacola to St. Mary's, examining with minute attention the various Keys or Islets on the margin of the coast. I have ascended many of the rivers, explored the lagoons and bays, traced the ancient improvements, scattered ruins, and its natural productions by land and by water." Hence the chief value of the work is as a gazetteer.

[1] The Territory of Florida; or Sketches of the Topography, Civil and Natural History of the Country, the Climate and the Indian Tribes, from the First Discovery to the Present Time. 8vo. New York, 1837.

The civil history is a mere compilation, collected without criticism, and arranged without judgment; an entire ignorance of other languages, and the paucity of materials in our own, incapacitated Williams from achieving anything more. Nor can he claim to be much of a naturalist, for the frequent typographical errors in the botanical names proclaim him largely debtor to others in this department. His style is eminently dry and difficult to labor through, and must ever confine the History to the shelf as a work of reference, and to the closet of the painful student. Yet with all its faults—and they are neither few nor slight—this is the most complete work ever published concerning the territory of Florida; it is the fruit of years of laborious investigation, of absorbing devotion to one object, often of keen mental and bodily suffering, and will ever remain a witness to the energy and zeal of its writer.

As little is recorded about this author pioneer, I may perhaps be excused for turning aside to recall a few personal recollections. It had long been my desire to visit and converse with him about the early days of the state, and with this object, on the 9th of November, 1856, I stopped at the little town of Picolati, near which he lived. A sad surprise awaited me; he had died on the 7th of the month and had been buried the day before my arrival. I walked through the woods to his house. It was a rotten, ruinous, frame tenement on the banks of the St. Johns, about half a mile below the town, fronted by a row of noble live oaks and surrounded by the forest. Here the old man—he was over eighty at the time of his death—had lived for twenty years almost entirely alone, and much of the time in abject poverty. A trader happened to be with him during his last illness, who told me some incidents of his history. His mind retained its vigor to the last, and within a week of his death he was actively employed in various literary avocations, among which was the preparation of an improved edition of his History, which he had very nearly completed. At the very moment the paralytic stroke, from which he died, seized him, he had the pen in his hand writing a novel, the scene of which was laid in China! His disposition was uncommonly aimable and engaging, and so much was he beloved by the Indians, that throughout the horrible atrocities of the Seminole war, when all the planters had fled or been butchered, when neither sex nor age was a protection, when Picolati was burned and St. Augustine threatened, he continued to live unharmed in his old house, though a companion was shot dead on the threshold. What the savage respected and loved, the civilized man thought weakness and despised; this very goodness of heart made him the object of innumerable petty impositions from the low whites, his neighbors. In the words of my informant, "he was too good for the people of these parts." During his lonely old age he solaced himself with botany and horticulture, priding himself on keeping the best garden in the vicinity. "Come, and I will show you his grave," said the trader, and added with a touch of feeling I hardly expected, "he left no directions about it, so I made it in the spot he used to love the best of all." He took me to the south-eastern corner of the neat garden plot. A heap of fresh earth with rough, round, pine sticks at head and foot, marked the spot. It was a solemn and impressive moment. The lengthening shadows of the forest crept over us, the wind moaned in the pines and whistled drearily through the sere grass, and the ripples of the river broke monotonously on the shore. All trace of the grave will soon be obliterated, the very spot forgotten, and the garden lie a waste, but the results of his long and toilsome life "in books recorded" will live when the marbles and monumental brasses of many of his cotemporaries shall be no more.

The next event that attracted general attention to Florida was the bloody and disastrous second Seminole war, which for deeds of atrocious barbarity, both on the part of the whites and red men, equals, if it does not surpass, any conflict that has ever stained the soil of our country.

The earliest work relative to it was published anonymously in 1836, by an officer in the army.[1] He gives an impartial account of the causes that gave rise to the war, the manifold insults and aggressions that finally goaded the Indians to desperation, and the incidents of the first campaign undertaken to punish them for their contumacy. It is well and clearly written, and coming from the pen of a participant in many of the scenes described, merits a place in the library of the historian.

The year subsequent, Mr. M. M. Cohen of Charleston, issued a notice of the proceedings in the peninsula.[2] He was an "officer of the left wing," and had spent about five months with the army, during which time it marched from St. Augustine to Volusia, thence to Tampa, and back again to St. Augustine. The

[1] The War in Florida; being an Exposition of its Causes and an accurate History of the Campaigns of Generals Gaines, Clinch and Scott. By a late Staff Officer. 8vo. Baltimore, 1836, pp. 184.

[2] History of the Florida Campaigns. 12mo. Charleston, 1837.

author tells us in his Preface, "our book has been put to press in less than thirty days from its being undertaken;" a statement no one will be inclined to doubt, as it is little more than a farrago of vapid puns and stale witticisms, hurriedly scraped together into a slim volume, and connected by a slender string of facts. An account of the imprisonment of Oceola and the enslavement of his wife, has been given by the same writer,[1] and has received praise for its accuracy.

In 1836, when the war was at its height, an Indian boy was taken prisoner by a party of American soldiers near Newnansville. Contrary to custom his life was spared, and the next year he was handed over to the care of an English gentleman then resident in the country. From his own account, drawn from him after long persuasion, his name was Nikkanoche, his father was the unhappy Econchatti-mico, and consequently he was nephew to the famous chief Oceola, (Ass-se-he-ho-lar, Rising Sun, Powell.) His guardian removed with him to England in 1840, and the year after his arrival there, published an account of the parentage, early days, and nation of his ward,[2] the young Prince of Econchatti, as he was styled. It forms an interesting and pleasant little volume, though I do not know what amount of reliance can be placed on the facts asserted.

An excellent article on the war, which merits careful reading from any one desirous of thoroughly sifting the question, may be found in the fifty-fourth volume of the North American Review, (1842,) prepared with

[1] In the Quarterly Anti-Slavery Magazine. (Giddings, Exiles of Florida, p. 99, note.)

[2] A Narrative of the Early Days and Remembrances of Oceola Nikkanoche, Prince of Econchatti, a young Seminole Indian. Written by his Guardian. 8vo. London, 1841, pp. 228.

reference to Mr. Horace Everett's remarks on the Army Appropriation Bill of July 14, 1840, and to a letter from the Secretary of War on the expenditure for supporting hostilities in Florida.

Though the above memoirs are of use in throwing additional light on some points, and settling certain mooted questions, the standard work of reference on the Florida war is the very able, accurate, and generally impartial History,[1] of Captain John T. Sprague, himself a participant in many of its scenes, and officially concerned in its prosecution. Few of our local histories rank higher than this. With a praiseworthy patience of research he goes at length into its causes, commencing with the cession in 1821, details minutely its prosecution till the close in December, 1845, and paints with a vigorous and skillful pen many of those thrilling adventures and affecting passages that marked its progress. A map of the seat of war that accompanies it, drawn up with care, and embracing most of the geographical discoveries made by the various divisions of the army, adds to its value.

Commencing his history with the cession, Captain Sprague does not touch on the earlier troubles with the Seminoles. These were never properly handled previous to the late work of the Hon. J. R. Giddings, entitled, "The Exiles of Florida."[2] These so-called exiles were runaway slaves from the colonies of South Carolina and Georgia, who, quite early in the last

1 The Origin, Progress, and Conclusion of the Florida War. 8vo. New York, 1848.

2 The Exiles of Florida; or, the Crimes Committed by our Government against the Maroons, who fled from South Carolina and other Slave States, seeking Protection under Spanish Laws. 8vo. Columbus, (Ohio,) 1858.

century, sought an asylum in the Spanish possessions, formed separate settlements, and, increased by fresh refugees, became ever after a fruitful source of broils and quarrels between the settlers of the rival provinces. As they were often protected, and by marriage and situation became closely connected with the Lower Creeks, they were generally identified with them in action under the common name of Seminoles. Thus the history of one includes that of the other. The profound acquaintance with the transactions of our government acquired by Mr. Giddings during a long and honorable public service, render his work an able plea in the cause of the people whose wrongs and sufferings have enlisted his sympathy; but unquestionably the fervor of his views prevents him from doing full justice to their adversaries. He attaches less weight than is right to the strict *legality* of most of the claims for slaves; and forgets to narrate the inhuman cruelties, shocking even to the red men, wreaked by these maroons on their innocent captives, which palliate, if they do not excuse, the rancorous hatred with which they were pursued by the whites. Including their history from their origin till 1853, the second Seminole war occupies much of his attention, and the treatment both of it and the other topics, prove the writer a capable historian, as well as an accomplished statesman.

It is unnecessary to specify the numerous reports of the officers, the official correspondence, the speeches of members of Congress, and other public writings that illustrate the history of the war, which are contained in the Executive Documents. But I should not omit to mention that the troubles in Florida during the last few years have given occasion to the publication of the only at all accurate description of the southern extremity of the peninsula in existence.[1] It was issued for the use of the army, from inedited reports of officers during the second Seminole war, and lays down and describes topographically nine routes to and from the principal military posts south of Tampa Bay.

The works relating to St. Augustine next claim our attention. Of late years this has become quite a favorite rendezvous for casual tourists, invalids from the north, magazine writers, *et id omne genus,* whence to indite letters redolent of tropic skies, broken ruins, balmy moonlight, and lustrous-eyed beauties. Though it would be lost time to enumerate these, yet among books of general travel, there are one or two of interest in this connection. Among these is an unpretending little volume that appeared anonymously at New York in 1839.[2] The author, a victim of asthma, had visited both St. Augustine and Key West in the spring of that year. Though written in a somewhat querulous tone, it contains some serviceable hints to invalids expecting to spend a winter in warmer climes.

Neither ought we to pass by in silence the Floridian notes of the "Hon. Miss Amelia M. Murray,"[3] who, it will be recollected, a few years since took a contemptuous glance at our country from Maine to Lousiana, weighed it in the balance of her judgment, and pronounced it wanting in most of the elements of

[1] Memoir to accompany a Military Map of Florida South of Tampa Bay, compiled by Lieutenant J. C. Ives, Topographical Engineer. War Department, April, 1856. 8vo. New York, 1856, pp. 42.

[2] A Winter in Florida and the West Indies. 12mo. New York, 1839.

[3] Letters from the United States, Canada and Cuba. New York, 1856.

civilization. She went on a week's scout into Florida, found the charges exorbitant, the government wretchedly conducted, and the people boors; was deeply disappointed with St. Augustine and harbor because an island shut out the view of the ocean, and at Silver Spring found nothing more worthy of her pen than the anti-slavery remark of an inn-keeper,—who has himself assured me that she entirely misconstrues even that.

Two works devoted to the Ancient City, as its inhabitants delight to style it, have been published. One of these is a pleasant little hand-book, issued some ten years since by the Rev. Mr. Sewall, Episcopalian minister there.[1] He prepared it "to meet the wants of those who may desire to learn something of the place in view of a sojourn, or who may have already come hither in search of health," and it is well calculated for this purpose. A view of the town from the harbor, (sold also separately,) and sketches of the most remarkable buildings increase its usefulness. A curious incident connected with this book is worth relating for the light it throws on the character of the so-called Minorcans of St. Augustine. In one part Mr. Sewall had inserted a passage somewhat depreciatory of this class. When the edition arrived and this became generally known, they formed a mob, surrounded the store where it was deposited, and could only be restrained from destroying the whole by a promise that the obnoxious leaf sould be cut from every volume in the package. This was done, and the copy I purchased there accordingly lacks the thirty-eighth and thirty-ninth pages.

[1] Sketches of St. Augustine, with a View of its History and Advantages as a Resort for Invalids. By R. K. Sewall. 8vo. New York, 1848, pp. 69.

An action on their part that calls to mind the ancient saw, "'Tis the tight shoe that pinches."

Another and later work that enters into the subject more at length, has recently appeared from the competent pen of G. R. Fairbanks,[1] a resident of the spot, and a close student of the chronicles of the old colony. The rise and progress of the settlements both French and Spanish are given in detail and with general accuracy, and though his account of the former is not so finished nor so thoroughly digested as that of Sparks, consisting of little more than extracts linked together, we have no other work in our language so full on the doings of the subjects of His Catholic Majesty in Florida, and the gradual growth of the Ancient City. It thus fills up a long standing hiatus in our popular historical literature.

Numerous articles on Florida have appeared in various American periodicals, but so few of any value that as a class they do not merit attention. Most of them are flighty descriptions of scenery, second-hand morsels of history, and empty political disquisitions. Some of the best I have referred to in connection with the points they illustrate, while the Index of Mr. Poole, a work invaluable to American scholars, obviates the necessity of a more extended reference.

Those that have appeared in the serials of Europe, on the other hand, as they mostly contain original matter, so they must not be passed over so lightly.

Though not strictly included among them, the article on Florida prepared by Mr. Warden for that portion of *L'Art de Verifier les Dates* called Historical

[1] The History and Antiquities of the City of St. Augustine, Florida, comprising some of the most Interesting Portions of the Early History of Florida. 8vo. New York, 1858.

Chronology of America, will come under our notice here. In a compendium parading such a pretentious title as this we have a right to expect at least an average accuracy, but this portion bears on its face obvious marks of haste, negligence, and a culpable lack of criticism, and is redeemed by nothing but a few excerpts from rare books.

Little attention has ever been paid to the natural history of the country, least of all by Americans. The best observer of late years has been M. de Castelnau, who, sent out by the Academie des Sciences to collect and observe in this department, spent in Middle Florida one of the seven years he passed in America. While the Seminole war was raging, and a mutual slaughter giving over the peninsula once more to its pristine wilderness, in the gloomy hammocks of the Suwannee and throughout the lofty forests that stretch between this river and the Apalachicola, this naturalist was pursuing his peaceful avocation undisturbed by the discord around him. In April, 1842, after his return, he submitted to the Academy a memoir on this portion of his investigations.[1] It is divided into three sections, the first a geographical description, the second treating of the climate, hygienic condition, geology, and agriculture, while the third is devoted to anthropology, as exhibited here in its three phases, the red, the white, and the black man. In one passage,[1] speaking of the history of the country, this author remarks that M. Lakanal "has, during his long sojourn at Mobile, just on the confines of Florida, collected numerous documents relative to the latter

[1] Memoire sur la Floride du Milieu, Comptes-Rendus, T. XIV., p. 518; T. XV., p. 1045.

[1] Comptes Rendus, XV., p. 1047.

country; but the important labors of our venerable colleague have not yet been published." As far as I can learn, these doubtless valuable additions to our history are still inedited.

The subjoined list of some other articles published in Europe is extracted from Dr. W. Koner's excellent catalogue.[1]

1832. De Mobile, Excursion dans l' Alabama et les Florides. Revue des Deux Mondes, T. I., p. 128.

1835. Beitrage zur Näheren Kenntniss von Florida. Anal. der Erdkunde, B. XII., s. 336.

1836. Castelnau, Note sur la Source de la Riviére de Walkulla dans la Floride. Soc. de Geographie, II ser., T. XI., p. 242.

1839. David, Aperçu Statistique sur la Floride Soc. de Geog., II, ser., Tom. XIV., p. 144.

1842. Castelnau, Note de deux Itineraîres de Charleston à Tallahassie. Soc. de Geog. T. XVIII, p. 241.

1843. Castelnau, Essai sur la Floride du Milieu. Annales de Voyages, T. IV, p. 129.

1843. De Quatrefages, La Floride. Revue des Deux Mondes, nouv. ser., T. I, p. 774.

§ 7.—Maps and Charts.

Though the need of a good history of the most important maps and charts of America, enriched by copies of the most interesting, cannot but have been felt by every one who has spent much time in the study of its first settlement and growth, such a work

[1] Repertorium ueber die - - - - auf dem Gebiete der Geschichte erscheinenen Aufsätze, u. s. w. Berlin, 1852.

still remains a desideratum in our literature. As a trifling aid to any who may hereafter engage in an undertaking of this kind, and as an assistance to the future historian of that portion of our country, I add a brief notice of those that best illustrate the progress of geographical knowledge respecting Florida.

On the earliest extant sketch of the New World—, that made by Juan de Cosa in 1500—, a continuous coast line running east and northeast connects the southern continent to the shores of the *Mar descubierta por Ingleses* in the extreme north. No signs of a peninsula are visible.

Eight year later, on the *Universalior cogniti Orbis Tabula* of Johannes Ruysch found in the geography of Ptolemy printed at Rome under the supervision of Marcus Beneventanus and Johannes Cotta, the whole of North America is included in a small body of land marked Terra Nova or Baccalauras,[1] joined to the countries of Gog and Magog and the *desertum Lob* in Asia. A cape stretching out towards Cuba is called Cabo de Portugesi.[2]

This brings us to the enigmatical map in the magnificent folio edition of Ptolemy, printed at Venice in 1513. On this, North America is an oblong parallelogram of land with an irregularly shaped portion projecting from its south-eastern extremity, maintaining with general correctness the outlines and direction of the peninsula of Florida. A number of capes and rivers are marked along its shores, some of the names evidently Portugese, others Spanish. Now as Leon

[1] *Bacalaos*, the Spanish word for codfish.

[2] See A. v. Humboldt's Introduction to Dr. T. W. Ghillany's Geschichte des Seefahrers Ritter Martin Behaim, s. 2—5, in which work these two maps are given.

first saw Florida in 1512, and the report of his discovery did not reach Europe for years, whence came this knowledge of the northern continent? Santarem and Ghillany both confess that there were voyages to the New World undertaken by Portuguese in the first decade of the century, about which all else but the mere fact of their existence have escaped the most laborious investigations; hence, probably to one of these unknown navigators we are to ascribe the honor of being the first discoverer of Florida, and the source of the information displayed by the editors of this copy of Ptolemy.[1]

The first outline of the coast drawn from known observation is the *Traza de las Costas de Tierra Firme y de las Tierras Nuevas*, accompanying the royal grant of those parts to Francisco de Garay in the year 1521. It has been published by Navarrete, and by Buckingham Smith. Contrary to the usual opinion of the day, which was not proved incorrect till the voyages of Francesco Fernandez de Cordova (1517), and more conclusively by that of Estevan Gomez (1525), the peninsula is attached to the mainland. This and other reasons render it probable that it was drawn up under the supervision of Anton de Alaminos, pilot of Leon on his first voyage, who ever denied the existence of an intervening strait.[2] I cannot agree with Mr. Smith that it points to any prior discoveries unknown to us.

[1] Many of the names on this map are also on the land called Terra de Cuba, north-west of the island Isabella, Cuba proper, on the globe of Johann Schoner, Nuremburg, 1520. A copy of a portion of the globe is given by Ghillany in the work just mentioned. For an inspection of the original maps of Ptolemy of 1508 and 1513, I am indebted to the kindness of Peter Force, of Washington.

[1] Otros conocieron ser tierra firme; y de este parecer fue

On some early maps, as one in the quarto geography of Ptolemy of 1525, the region of Florida is marked Parias. This name, originally given by Columbus to an island of the West Indian archipelago, and so laid down on the "figura ò pintura de la tierra," which he forwarded to Ferdinand the Catholic in 1499,[1] was quite wildly applied by subsequent geographers to Peru, to the region on the shore of the Caribbean Sea, to the whole of South America, to the southern extremity of North America where Nicaragua now is, and finally to the peninsula of Florida.

We have seen that early maps prove De Leon was not, as is commonly supposed, the first to see and name the Land of Flowers (Terra Florida); neither did his discoveries first expand a knowledge of it in Europe. Probably all that was known by professed geographers regarding it for a long time after was the product of later explorations, for not till forty years from the date of his first voyage was there a chart published containing the name he applied to the peninsula. This is the one called *Novae Insulae,* in the Geographia Claudii Ptolemaei, Basileae, 1552.[2]

The only other delineation of the country dating from the sixteenth century that deserves notice—for those of Herrera are quite worthless—is that by Jacques Le Moyne de Morgues, published in the second volume of De Bry, which is curious as the only one left by the French colonists, though geographically

siempre Anton de Alaminos, Piloto, que fue con Juan Ponce. Barcia, Introduccion al Ensayo Chronologico.

[1] Herrera, Dec. I., Lib. I., cap. iii., p. 91.

[2] For a description of this and other maps of America during the sixteenth century, see Dr. Ghillany, ubi suprà, p. 58, Anmerk. 17.

not more correct than others of the day. Indeed, all of them portray the country very imperfectly. Generally it is represented as a triangular piece of land more or less irregular, indented by bays, divided into provinces Cautio, Calos, Tegeste, and others, names which are often applied to the whole peninsula. The southern extremity is sometimes divided into numerous islands by arms of the sea, and the St. Johns, when down at all, rises from mountains to the north, and runs in a southeasterly direction, nearly parallel with the rivers supposed to have been discovered by Ribaut, (La Somme, La Loire, &c.)

Now this did not at all keep pace with the geographical knowledge common to both French and Spanish towards the close of this period. The colonists under Laudonniére and afterwards Aviles himself, ascended the St. Johns certainly as far as Lake George, and knew of a great interior lake to the south; Pedro Menendez Marquez, the nephew and successor of the latter, made a methodical survey of the coast from Pensacola to near the Savannah river (from Santa Maria de Galve to Santa Helena;) and English navigators were acquainted with its general outline and the principal points along the shore.

Yet during the whole of the next century I am not aware of a single map that displays any signs of improvement, or any marks of increased information. That inserted by De Laet in his description of the New World, called *Florida et Regiones Vicinæ*, (1633,) is noteworthy only because it is one of the first, if not the first, to locate along his supposed route the native towns and provinces met with by De Soto. Their average excellence may be judged from those inserted in the elephantine work of Ogilby on America, (1671,) and still better in its Dutch and German paraphrases. The *Totius Americæ Descriptio,* by Gerhard a Schagen in the latter, is a meritorious production for that age.

No sooner, however, had the English obtained a firm footing in Carolina and Georgia, and the French in Louisiana, than a more accurate knowledge of their Spanish neighbors was demanded and acquired. The "New Map of ye North Parts of America claimed by France under ye name of Louisiana, Mississippi, Canada, and New France, with ye adjoining Territories of England and Spain," (London, 1720,) indicates considerable progress, and is memorable as the first on which the St. Johns is given its true course, information about which its designer Herman Moll, obtained from the "Journals and Original Draughts" of Captain Nairn. His map of the West Indies contains a "Draught of St. Augustine and its Harbour," with the localities of the castle, town, monastery, Indian church, &c., carefully pointed out; previous to it, two plans of this city had appeared, one, the earliest extant, engraved to accompany the narrative of Drake's Voyage and Descent in 1586, and another, I know not by whose hand, representing its appearance in 1665.[1]

On the former of these maps, "The South Bounds of Carolina," are placed nearly a degree south of St. Augustine, thus usurping all the best portion of the Spanish territory. This is but an example of the great confusion that prevailed for a long time as to the extent of the region called Florida. The early

[1] See G. R. Fairbanks, History and Antiquities of St. Augustine, pp. 113, 130, for descriptions of the two latter. A "Geog. Description of Florida" is said to have appeared at London, in 1665. Possibly it is the account of Captain Davis' attack upon St. Augustine.

writers frequently embraced under this name the whole of North America above Mexico, distinguishing, as Herrera and Torquemada, between Florida explored and unexplored, (Florida conocida, Florida ignorada,) or as Christian Le Clerq, between Spanish and French and English Florida. Taking it in this extended sense, Barcia includes in his Chronology (Ensayo Cronologico de la Florida) not only the operations of the Spanish and English on the east coast of the United States, but also those of the French in Canada and the expeditions of Vasquez Coronado and others in New Mexico. Nicolas le Fer, on the other hand, ignoring the name altogether, styled the whole region Louisiana, (1718,) while the English, not to be outdone in national rapacity, laid claim to an equal amount as Carolina. De Laet[1] was the first geographer who confined the name to the peninsula. In 1651 Spain relinquished her claims to all land north of 36° 30′ north lat., but it was not till the Definitive Treaty of Peace of 1763, that any political attempt was made to define its exact boundaries, and then, not with such entire success, but room was left for subsequent disputes between our government and Spain, only finally settled by the surveys of Ellicott at the close of the century.

Neither Guillaume de l'Isle nor M. Bellin, both of whom etched maps of Florida many years after the publication of that of Moll, seems to have been aware of his previous labors, or to have taken advantage of his more extensive information. In the gigantic *Atlas Nouveau* of the former, (Amsterdam, 1739,) are two maps of Florida, evidently by different hands. The one, *Tabula Geographica Mexico et Floridæ,* gives toler-

[1] Descriptio Indiæ Occidentalis, Lib. IV., cap. xiii. (Antwerpt, 1633.)

ably well the general contour of the peninsula, and situates the six provinces of Apalacha mentioned by Bristock; the other, *Carte de la Louisiane et du Cours du Mississippi*, is an enlarged copy with additions of that published five years previous in the fifth volume of the *Voyages au Nord*, on which is given the route of De Soto. Bellin's *Carte des Costes de la Nouvelle France suivant les premiéres Decouvertes* is found in Charlevoix's *Nouvelle France* and is of little worth.

The map of "Carolina, Florida, and the Bahama Islands," that accompanies Catesby's Natural History of those regions, is not so accurate as we might expect from the opportunities he enjoyed. The peninsula is conceived as a nearly equilateral triangle projecting about two hundred and sixty miles towards the south. Like other maps of this period, it derives its chief value from locating Indian and Spanish towns.

The dangerous navigation of the Keys had necessitated their examination at an early date. In 1718, Domingo Gonzales Carranza surveyed them, as well as some portion of the northern coast, with considerable care. His notes remained in manuscript, however, till 1740, when falling into the hands of an Englishman, they were translated and brought out at London under the title, "A Geographical Description of the Spanish West Indies." But how inefficient the knowledge of these perilous reefs remained for many years is evident on examining the marine chart of the Gulf of Mexico, by Tomas Lopez and Juan de la Cruz, in 1755. The seafaring English, when they took possession of the country, made it their first duty to get the most exact possible charts of these so important points. No sooner had the treaty been signed than the Board of Admiralty dispatched G. Gauld, a capable and energetic engineer to survey the coasts, islands, and keys, east and south of Pensacola. In this employment he spent nearly twenty years, from 1764 to 1781, when he was taken prisoner by the Spanish, and shortly afterwards died. The results were not made public till 1790, when they appeared under the supervision of Dr. Lorimer, and, in connection with the Gulf Pilot of Bernard Romans, and the sailing directions of De Brahm, both likewise engineers in the British service, employed at the same time as Gauld, constituted for half a century the chief foundation for the nautical charts of this entrance to the Gulf.

Among the writers of the last century who did good service to American geography, Thomas Jefferys, Geographer to his Majesty, deserves honorable mention. Besides his more general labors, he edited, in 1763, the compilation of Roberts, and some years after the Journal of the elder Bartram; to both he added a general map of the region under consideration, "collected and digested with great care and labor from a number of French and Spanish charts," taken on prize ships, correct enough as far as regards the shore, but the interior very defective; a plan of Tampa Bay; and one of St. Augustine and harbor, giving the depth of water in each, and on the latter showing the site of the sea wall.

Besides those in the Atlas of Popple, of 1772, the following maps, published during the last century, may be consulted with advantage:

Carolinæ, Floridæ nec-non Insularum Bajamensium delineatio, Nuremberg, 1775.

Tabulæ Mexicanæ et Floridæ, terrarum Anglicarum, anteriarum Americæ insularum. Amstelodami, apud Petrum Schenck, circ. 1775.

A Map of the Southern British Colonies, containing

the Seat of War in N. and S. Carolina, E. and W. Florida. By Bernard Romans. London, 1776.

Plan of Amelia Island and Bar, surveyed by Jacob Blaney in 1775. London, 1776.

Plan of Amelia Island and Bar. By Wm. Fuller. Edited by Thomas Jefferys. London, 1776.

Plano de la Ciudad y Puerto de San Augustin de la Florida. Por Tomas Lopez. Madrid, 1783.

Nothing was done of any importance in this department during the second Spanish supremacy, but as soon as the country became a portion of the United States, the energy both of private individuals and the government rapidly increased the fund of geographical knowledge respecting it.

The first map published was that of Vignoles, who, an engineer himself, and deriving his facts from a personal survey of the whole eastern coast from St. Marys river to Cape Florida, makes a very visible improvement on his predecessors.

The canal contemplated at this period from the St. Johns or St. Marys to the Gulf gave occasion to levellings across the peninsula at two points, valuable for the hypsometrical data they furnish. Annexed to the report (February, 1829,) is a "Map of the Territory of Florida from its northern boundary to lat. 27° 30′ N. connected with the delta of the Mississippi," giving the features of the country and separate plans of the harbors and bays.

The same year J. R. Searcy issued a map of the territory, "constructed principally from authentic documents in the land office at Tallahassie," favorably mentioned at the time.[1]

[1] Southern Review, Vol. VI., p. 410, seq.

The map prefixed to his View of West Florida, and subsequently to his later work, by Colonel Williams, largely based on his own researches, is a good exposition of all certainly known at that period about the geography of the country. Cape Romans is here first distinguished as an island; Sharks river is omitted; and Lake Myaco or Okee-chobee is not down, "simply," says the author, "because I can find no reason for believing its existence!" Unparalleled as such an entire ignorance of a body of water with a superficies of twelve hundred square miles, in the midst of a State settled nigh half a century before any other in our Union, which had been governed for years by English, by Spanish, and by Americans, may be, it well illustrates the impassable character of those vast swamps and dense cypresses known as the Everglades; an impenetrability so complete as almost to justify the assertion of the State engineer, made as late as 1855: "These lands are now, and will continue to be, nearly as much unknown as the interior of Africa or the mountain sources of the Amazon."[1]

What little we know of this Terra Incognita, is derived from the notes of officers in the Indian wars, and the maps drawn up for the use of the army. Among these, that issued by the War Department at the request of General Taylor, in 1837, embracing the whole peninsula, that prefixed to Sprague's History, which gives the northern portion with much minuteness, and the later one, in 1856, of the portion south of Tampa Bay, are the most important. The latter gives the topography of the Everglades and Big Cypress as far as ascertained.

[1] Report of F. L. Dancy, State Engineer and Geologist, in the Message of the Governor of Florida, with Accompanying Documents, for 1855, App., p. 9.

While annual explorations are thus throwing more and more light on the interior of the peninsula, the United States Coast Survey, now in operation, will definitely settle all kindred questions relative to its shores, harbors, and islands; and thus we may look forward to a not distant day when its geographical history will be consummated.

CHAPTER II.

THE APALACHES.

Derivation of the name.—Earliest notices of.—Visited and described by Bristock in 1653.—Authenticity of his narrative.—Subsequent history and final extinction.

AMONG the aboriginal tribes of the United States perhaps none is more enigmatical than the Apalaches. They are mentioned as an important nation by many of the early French and Spanish travellers and historians, their name is preserved by a bay and river on the shores of the Gulf of Mexico, and by the great eastern coast range of mountains, and has been applied by ethnologists to a family of cognate nations that found their hunting-grounds from the Mississippi to the Atlantic and from the Ohio river to the Florida Keys; yet, strange to say, their own race and place have been but guessed at. Intimately connected both by situation and tradition with the tribes of the Floridian peninsula, an examination of the facts pertaining to their history and civilization is requisite to a correct knowledge of the origin and condition of the latter.

The orthography of the name is given variously by the older writers, Apahlahche, Abolachi, Apeolatei, Appallatta, &c., and very frequently without the first letter, Palaxy, Palatcy. Daniel Coxe, indeed, fancifully considered this first vowel the Arabic article *a*, *al*, prefixed by the Spaniards to the native word.[1] Its derivation has been a *questio vexata* among Indianologists; Heckewelder[2] identified it with Lenape or Wapanaki, "which name the French in the south as easily corrupted into *Apalaches* as in the north to *Abenakis*," and other writers have broached equally loose hypothesis. Adair[3] mentions a Chikasah town, Palacheho, evidently from the same root; but it is not from this tongue nor any of its allies, that we must explain its meaning, but rather consider it an indication of ancient connections with the southern continent, and in itself a pure Carib word. *Apáliché* in the Tamanaca dialect of the Guaranay stem on the Orinoco signifies *man*,[4] and the earliest application of the name in the northern continent was as a title of the chief of a country, *l'homme par excellence*,[5] and hence, like very many other Indian tribes (Apaches, Lenni Lenape, Illinois,) his subjects assumed by eminence the proud appellation of The Men. How this foreign word came to be imported will be considered hereafter. Among the tribes that made up the confederacy, probably only one partook of the warring and energetic blood of the Caribs; or it may have been assumed in emulation of a famous neighbor; or it may have been a title of honor derived

[1] A Description of the Province of Carolina, p. 2, London, 1727.

[2] Trans. Hist. and Lit. Com. of the Am. Phil. Soc., Vol. I., p. 113.

[3] Hist. of the American Indians, p. 353.

[4] Gilii' Saggio di Storia Americana, Tomo III., p. 375.

[5] Rex qui in hisce Montibus habitabat, Ao. 1562, dicabatur Apalatcy; ideoque ipsi montes eodem nomine vocantur, is written on the map of the country in Dapper's Neue und Unbekante Welt (Amsterdam, 1673,) probably on the authority of Ribaut.

from the esoteric language of a foreign priesthood, instances of which are not rare among the aborigines.

In the writings of the first discoverers they uniformly hold a superior position as the most polished, the most valorous, and the most united tribe in the region where they dwelt. The fame of their intrepidity reached to distant nations. "Keep on, robbers and traitors," cried the Indians near the Withlacooche to the soldiers of De Soto, "in Apalache you will receive that chastisement your cruelty deserves." When they arrived at this redoubted province they found cultivated fields stretching on either hand, bearing plentiful crops of corn, beans, pumpkins, cucumbers, and plums,[1] whose possessors, a race large in stature, of great prowess, and delighting in war, inhabited numerous villages containing from fifty to three hundred spacious and commodious dwellings, well protected against hostile incursions. The French colonists heard of them as distinguished for power and wealth, having good store of gold, silver, and pearls, and dwelling near lofty mountains to the north; and Fontanedo, two years a prisoner in their power, lauds them as "*les meilleurs Indiens de la Floride*," and describes their province as stretching far northward to the snow-covered mountains of Onagatano abounding in precious metals.[2]

About a century subsequent to these writers, we find a very minute and extraordinary account of a

[1] The plums mentioned by these writers were probably the fruit of the Prunus Chicasaw. This was not an indigenous tree, but was cultivated by the Southern tribes. During his travels, the botanist Bartram never found it wild in the forests, "but always in old deserted Indian plantations." (Travels, p. 38.)

[2] See Appendix III.

nation called Apalachites, indebted for its preservation principally to the work of the Abbé Rochefort. It has been usually supposed a creation of his own fertile brain, but a careful study of the subject has given me a different opinion. The original sources of his information may be entirely lost, but that they actually existed can be proved beyond reasonable doubt. They were a series of ephemeral publications by an "English gentleman" about 1656, whose name is variously spelled Bristol, Bristok, Brigstock, and Bristock, the latter being probably the correct orthography. He had spent many years in the West Indies and North America, was conversant with several native tongues, and had visited Apalacha in 1653. Besides the above-mentioned fragmentary notes, he promised a complete narrative of his residence and journeys in the New World, but apparently never fulfilled his intention. Versions of his account are found in various writers of the age. The earliest is given by Rochefort,[1] and was translated with the rest of the work of that author by Davies,[2] who must have consulted the original tract of Bristock as he adds particulars not found in the Abbé's history. Others are met with in the writings of the Geographus Ordinarius, Nicolas Sanson d' Abbeville,[3] in the huge tomes of Ogilby[4] and his high and low

[1] Histoire Naturelle et Morale des Illes Antilles de l'Amerique, Liv. II., pp. 331–353. Rotterdam, 1658.

[2] History of the Caribby Islands, London, 1666.

[3] Geographia Exactissima, oder Beschreibung des 4 Theil der ganzen Welt mit Geographischen und Historischen Relationen, Franckfort am Mayn, 1679. This is a German translation of D'Abbeville's geographical essays. I have not been able to learn when the last part, which contains Bristock's narrative, was published in French.

[4] America. London, 1671.

Dutch paraphrasers Arnoldus Montanus[1] and Oliver Dapper,[2] in Oldmixon's history,[3] quite fully in the later compilation that goes under the name of Baumgarten's History of America,[4] and in our own days has been adverted to by the distinguished Indianologist H. R. Schoolcraft in more than one of his works. It consists of two parts, the one treating of the traditions, the other of the manners and customs of the Apalachites. In order to place the subject in the clearest light I shall insert a brief epitome of both.

The Apalachites inhabited the region called Apalacha between 33° 25′ and 37° north latitude. By tradition and language they originated from northern Mexico, where similar dialects still existed.[5] The Cofachites were a more southern nation, scattered at first over the vast plains and morasses to the south along the Gulf of Mexico (Theomi), but subsequently having been reduced by the former nation, they settled a district called Amana, near the mountains of Apalacha, and from this circumstance received the name Caraibe or Carib, meaning "bold, warlike men," "strangers," and "annexed nation." In after days, increasing in strength and retaining their separate ex-

[1] De Nieuwe en Onbekeende Weereld. Amsterdam, 1671.

[2] Die Unbekante Neue Welt. Amsterdam, 1673.

[3] The British Empire in America, Vol. I. London, 1708.

[4] Geschichte von Amerika, B. II. Halle, 1753. The articles in these volumes were selected with much judgment, and translated by J. F. Geyfarts and J. F. Schrœter, Baumgarten merely writing the bibliographical introductions. It contains a curious map entitled *Gegend der Provinz Bemarin im Königreich Apalacha.*

[5] The Chikasah asserted for themselves the same origin, and èven their Mexican relatives were said to visit them from time to time. (Adair, Hist. of the North Am. Indians, p. 195.)

istence, they asserted independence, refused homage to the king of Apalacha, and slighted the worship of the sun. Wars consequently arose, extending at intervals over several centuries, resulting in favor of the Cofachites, whose dominion ultimately extended from the mountains in the north to the shores of the Gulf and the river St. Johns on the south. Finding themselves too weak to cope openly with such a powerful foe, the Apalachites had recourse to stratagem. Taking advantage of a temporary peace, their priests used the utmost exertions to spread abroad among their antagonists a religious veneration of the sun and a belief in the necessity of an annual pilgrimage to his sacred mountain Olaimi in Apalacha. So well did their plan succeed, that when at the resumption of hostilities, the Apalachites forbade the ingress of all pilgrims but those who would do homage to their king, a schism, bitter and irreconcileable, was brought about among the Cofachites. Finally peace was restored by a migration of those to whom liberty was dearer than religion, and a submission of the rest to the Apalachites, with whom they became amalgamated and lost their identity. Their more valiant companions, after long wanderings through unknown lands in search of a home, finally locate themselves on the southern shore of Florida. Islanders from the Bahamas, driven thither by storms, tell them of lands, fertile and abounding in game, yet uninhabited and unclaimed, lying to the southwards; they follow their advice and direction, traverse the Gulf of Florida, and settle the island of *Ayay*, now Santa Cruz. From this centre colonies radiated, till the majority of the islands and no small portion of the southern mainland was peopled by their race.

Such is the sum of Bristock's singular account. It is either of no credibility whatever, or it is a distorted version of floating, dim traditions, prevalent among the indigenes of the West Indies and the neighboring parts of North America. I am inclined to the latter opinion, and think that Bristock, hearing among the Caribs rumors of a continent to the north, and subsequently finding powerful nations there, who, in turn, knew of land to the south and spoke of ancient wars and migrations, wove the fragments together, filled up the blanks, and gave it to the world as a veritable history. To support this view, let us inquire whether any knowledge of each other actually existed between the inhabitants of the islands and the northern mainland, and how far this knowledge extended.

The reality of the migration, though supported by some facts, must be denied of the two principal races, the Caribs and Arowauks, who peopled the islands at the time of their discovery. The assertions of Barcia, Herrera, and others that they were originally settled by Indians from Florida have been abundantly disproved by the profound investigations of Alphonse D' Orbigny in South America.[1] On the other hand, that the Cubans and Lucayans had a knowledge of the peninsula not only in the form of myths but as a real geographical fact, even having specific names in their own tongues for it (Cautio, Jaguaza), is declared by the unanimous voice of historians.

[1] Numerous references showing the prevalence of this error are adduced by D'Orbigny, L'Homme Americain, Tom. II., p. 275, et seq. Among later authors who have been misled by such authorities are Humboldt, ("Reise nach dem Tropen, B. V., s. 181,") and the eminent naturalist F. J. F. Meyen, (Ueber die Ur-Eingebornen von Peru, s. 6, in the Nov. Act. Acad. Cæsar. Leopold. Carolin. Nat. Cur. Vol. XVII., Sup. I.)

The most remarkable of these myths was that of the fountain of life, placed by some in the Lucayos, but generally in a fair and genial land to the north.[1] From the tropical forests of Central America to the coral-bound Antilles the natives told the Spaniards marvellous tales of a fountain whose magic waters would heal the sick, rejuvenate the aged, and confer an ever-youthful immortality. It may have originated in a confused tradition of a partial derivation from the mainland and subsequent additions thence received from time to time, or more probably from the adoration of some of the very remarkable springs abundant on the peninsula, perchance that wonderful object the Silver Spring,[2] round which I found signs of a dense

[1] Writers disagree somewhat as to the situation of this fountain. Hackluyt (Vol. V., p. 251) and Gomara (Hist. de las Indias Occidentales, Cap XLV., pp. 31, 35) locate it on the island Boiuca or Agnaneo, 125 leagues north of Hispaniola. Some placed it on the island Bimini,—which, says Oviedo, is 40 leagues west of Bahama (Pt. I., lib. xix., cap. xv., quoted in Navarrete,)—a name sometimes applied to Florida itself, as on the Chart of Cristobal de Topia given in the third volume of Navarrete. Herrera, La Vega, Fontanedo, Barcia, Navarrete and most others agree in referring it to Florida. Fontanedo confuses it with the river Jordan and the Espiritu Santo or Mississippi. Gomara (ubi suprà, p. 31) gives a unique interpretation to this myth and one quite in accordance with the Spanish character, namely, that it arose from the rare beauty of the women of that locality, which was so superlative that old men, gazing upon it, would feel themselves restored to the vigor of youth. In this he is followed by Ogilby. (America, p. 344.)

[2] See Appendix I. The later Indians of Florida seem to have preserved certain relics of a superstitious veneration of the aqueous element. Their priests had a certain *holy water*, sanctified by blowing upon it and incantation, thought to possess healing virtues (Nar. of Oceola Nikkanoche, p. 141;) Coacooche said that when the spirit of his twin-sister came to him from the land of souls, she offered him a cup of pure

early population, its virtues magnified by time, distance, and the arts of priests. We know how intimately connected is the worship of the sun with the veneration of water; heat typifying the masculine, moisture the feminine principle. The universality of their association in the Old World cosmogonies and mythologies is too well-known to need specification, and it is quite as invariable in those of the New Continent. That such magnificent springs as occur in Florida should have become objects of special veneration, and their fame bruited far and wide, and handed down form father to son, is a most natural consequence in such faiths.[1]

Certain it is that long before these romantic tales had given rise to the expeditions of De Leon, Narvaez, and De Soto, many natives of the Lucayos, of Cuba, even of Yucatan and Honduras,[2] had set out in search of this mystic fount. Many were lost, while some lived to arrive on the Floridian coast, where finding it impossible either to proceed or return, they formed small villages, "whose race," adds Barcia,[3] writing in

water, "which she said came from the spring of the Great Spirit, and if I should drink of it, I should return and live with her for ever." (Sprague, Hist. Florida War, p. 328.)

[1] Parallel myths are found in various other nations. Sir John Maundeville speaks of the odoriferous fountain of youth near the river Indus, and Ellis mentions "the Hawaiian account of the voyage of Kamapiikai to the land where the inhabitants enjoy perpetual health, where the *wai ora* (life-giving fountain) removed every internal malady and external deformity or decrepitude from those who were plunged beneath its salutary waters." (Polynesian Researches, Vol I., p. 103.)

[2] Fontanedo, Memoire, pp. 17, 18, 19, 32, 39. Gomara, Hist. de las Indias, cap. XLI., p. 31.

[3] Intro. to the Ensay. Cron.; Fontanedo makes the same statement.

1722, "is still in existence" (cuia generacion aun dura). This statement, which the cautious investigator Navarrete confirms,[1] seems less improbable when we reflect that in after times it was no uncommon incident for the natives of Cuba to cross the Gulf of Florida in their open boats to escape the slavery of the Spaniards,[2] that the Lucayans had frequent communication with the mainland,[3] that the tribes of South Florida, as early as 1695, carried on a considerable trade with Havana,[4] that the later Indians on the Suwannee would on their trading excursions not only descend this river in their large cypress canoes, but proceed "quite to the point of Florida, and sometimes cross the Gulph, extending their navigations to the Bahama islands and even to Cuba,"[5] and finally that nothing was more common to such a seafaring nation as the Caribs than a voyage of this length.[6]

Another remarkable myth, which certainly points for its explanation to an early and familiar intercourse between the islands and the mainland, is the singular

[1] Despues de establecido los Españoles en las Islas de Santo Domingo, Cuba, y Puerto Rico, averiguaron que los naturales conservaban algunas ideas vagas de tierras situadas à la parte septentrional, donde èntre otras cosas maravillosas referian la existencia de cierta fuente y rio, cuyas aguas remozaban à los viejos que en ella se bañaban ; preocupacion tan añeja y arraigada en los Indios, que aun antes de la llegada de los españoles los habia conducido à establecer allì una colonia. Viages y Descubrimientos, Tomo III., p. 60.

[2] L'Art de Verifier les Dates, Chronologie Historique de l'Amerique, Tome VIII., p. 185.

[3] Herrera, Dec. I., Lib. IX., cap. XI., p. 249.

[4] Barcia, Ensay. Cron., Año 1698, p. 317, Careri, Voyage round the World, in Churchill's Coll. Vol. IV., p. 537.

[5] William Bartram, Travels, p. 227.

[6] See Labat, Voyage aux Isles de l'Amerique, Tome I., p. 136, and Hughes, Nat. Hist of Barbadoes, p. 5.

geognostic tradition prevalent among the Lucayans, preserved by Peter of Anghiera, to the effect that this archipelago was originally united to the continent by firm land.[1] Doubtless it was on such grounds that the Spaniards concluded that they owed their original settlement to migrations from the Floridian peninsula.

Turning our attention now to this latter land, we should have cause to be surprised did we not find signs that such adventurous navigators as the Caribs had planned and executed incursions and settlements there. That these signs are so sparse and unsatisfactory we owe not so much to their own rarity as to the slight weight attached to such things by the early explorers and discoverers. From the accounts we do possess, however, there can be no doubt but that vestiges of the Caribbean tongue, if not whole tribes identical with them in language and customs, have been met with from time to time on the peninsula.[2] The striking similarity in the customs of flattening the forehead, in poisoning weapons, in the use of hollow reeds to propel arrows, in the sculpturing on war clubs, construction of dwellings, exsiccation of corpses,[3]

[1] Jucaias a conjecturis junctas fuisse quondam reliquis magnis insulis nostri arbitrantur, et ita fuisee a suis majoribus creditum incolæ fatentur. Sed vi tempestate paulatim absorpta tellure alterne secessisse, pelago interjecto uti de messenensi freto est autorum opinio Siciliam ab Italia dirimente, quod una esset quondam contigua. De Novo Orbe, Dec. VII., cap. II., p. 468, Editio Hackluyti, Parisiis, 1587.

[2] On this topic consult Baumgarten, Geschichte von Amerika, B. II., s. 583; Jefferys, Hist of the French Dominion in America, Pt. II., p. 181; Adelung, Allgemeine Sprachenkunde, Th. II., Ab. II., s. 681; Barton, New Views of the Tribes of America, p. lxxi.; Hervas, Catalogo de las Lenguas conocidas, Tomo I., p. 387.

[3] See Appendix II.

burning the houses of the dead, and other rites, though far from conclusive are yet not without a decided weight. It is much to be regretted that Adair has left us no fuller information of those seven tribes on the Koosah river, who spoke a different tongue from the Muskohge and preserved "a fixed oral tradition that they formerly came from South America, and after sundry struggles in defence of liberty settled their present abode."[1]

Thus it clearly appears that the frame, so to speak, of the traditions preserved by Bristock actually did exist and may be proved from other writers. But we are still more strongly convinced that his account is at least founded on fact, when we compare the manners and customs of the Apalachites, as he gives them, with those of the Cherokee, Choktah, Chickasah, and Muskohge, tribes plainly included by him under this name, and proved by the philological researches of Gallatin to have occupied the same location since De Soto's expedition.[2] We need have no suspicion that he plagiarized from other authors, as the particulars he mentions are not found in earlier writers; and it was not till 1661 that the English settled Carolina, not till 1699 that Iberville built his little fort on the Bay of Biloxi, and many years elapsed between this latter and the general treaty of Oglethorpe. If then we find a close similarity in manners, customs, and religions, we must perforce concede his accounts, such as they have reached us, a certain degree of credit.

1 Hist. of the North Am. Indians, p. 267.

2 Trans. Am Antiq. Soc. Vol. II., p. 103 seq. Bossu found the tradition of De Soto's invasion rife among the Alibamons (Creeks) of his day. (Nouv. Voyages aux Indes Occident. Pt. II., pp. 34, 35. Paris, 1768.)

He begins by stating that Apalacha was divided into six provinces; Dumont,[1] writing from independent observation about three-fourths of a century afterwards, makes the same statement. Their towns were inclosed with stakes or live hedges, the houses built of stakes driven into the ground in an oval shape, were plastered with mud and sand, whitewashed without, and some of a reddish glistening color within from a peculiar kind of sand, thatched with grass, and only five or six feet high, the council-house being usually on an elevation.[2] If the reader will turn to the authorities quoted in the subjoined note, he will find this an exact description of the towns and single dwellings of the later Indians.[3] The women manufactured mats of down and feathers with the same skill that a century later astonished

[1] Memoires Historiques sur la Louisiane, Tome II., p. 301.

[2] The Cherokees plastered their houses both roofs and walls inside and out with clay and dried grass, and to compensate for the lowness of the walls excavated the floor as much as three or four feet. From this it is probable they were the "Indi delle Vacche" of Cabeza de Vaca "tra queste case ve ne havea alcune che erano di terra, e tutte l'altre sono di stuore." (Di Alvaro Nunnes Relatione in Ramusio, Viaggi, Tom. III., fol. 327, B.) A similar construction was noticed by Biedma in Acapachiqui where the houses "etaient creusées sous terre et rassemblaient à des cavernes," (Relation, pp. 60, 61,) by the Portuguese Gentlemen in Capachiqui, (Hackluyt, Vol. V., p. 498.) and by La Vega among the Cofachiqui, (Conq. de la Florida, Lib. III., cap. XV., p. 181.) Hence the Cherokees are identical with the latter and not with the Achalaques, as Schoolcraft erroneously advances. (Thirty Years with the Indian Tribes, p. 595.) I suppose it was from this peculiar style of building that the Iroquois called them *Owaudah*, a people who live in caves. (Schoolcraft, Notes on the Iroquois, p. 163.)

[3] Adair, Hist. of the N. Am. Inds., pp. 413, 420, 421; Wm. Bartram, Travels, pp. 367, 388; Le Page Dupratz, Hist. of Louisiana, Vol. II., pp. 351–2.

Adair,[1] and spun like these the wild hemp and the mulberry bark into various simple articles of clothing. The fantastic custom of shaving the hair on one-half the head, and permitting the other half to remain, on certain emergencies, is also mentioned by later travellers.[2] Their food was not so much game as peas, beans, maize, and other vegetables, produced by cultivation; and the use of salt obtained from vegetable ashes, so infrequent among the Indians, attracted the notice of Bristock as well as Adair.[3] Their agricultural character reminds us of the Choktahs, among whom the men helped their wives to labor in the field, and whom Bernard Romans[4] called "a nation of farmers." In Apalache, says Dumont,[5] "we find a less rude, more refined nation, peopling its meads and fertile vales, cultivating the earth, and living on the abundance of excellent fruit it produces."

Strange as a fairy tale is Bristock's description of their chief temple and the rites of their religion—of the holy mountain Olaimi lifting its barren, round summit far above the capital city Melilot at its base—of the two sacred caverns within this mount, the innermost two hundred feet square and one hundred in height, wherein were the emblematic vase ever filled with crystal water that trickled from the rock, and the "grand altar" of one round stone, on which incense, spices, and aromatic shrubs were the only offerings—of the platform, sculptured from the solid rock, where

[1] Hist. N. Am. Inds., pp. 422–3.

[2] François Coreal, Voyages, Tome I., p. 31; Catesby, Account of Florida and the Bahama Islands, p. viii.

[3] Hist. N. Am. Inds., p. 116.

[4] Nat. Hist. of E. and W. Florida, pp. 71, 83.

[5] Mems. Hist. sur la Louisiane, Tome II., p. 301.

the priests offered their morning orisons to the glorious orb of their divinity at his daily birth—of their four great annual feasts—all reminding us rather of the pompous rites of Persian or Peruvian heliolatry than the simple sun worship of the Vesperic tribes. Yet in essentials, in stated yearly feasts, in sun and fire worship, in daily prayers at rising and setting sun, in frequent ablution, we recognize through all this exaggeration and coloring, the religious habits that actually prevailed in those regions. Indeed, the speculative antiquarian may ask concerning Mount Olaimi itself, whether it may not be identical with the enormous mass of granite known as "The Stone Mountain" in De Kalb county, Georgia, whose summit presents an oval, flat, and naked surface two or three hundred yards in width, by about twice that in length, encircled by the remains of a mural construction of unknown antiquity, and whose sides are pierced by the mouths of vast caverns;[1] or with Lookout mountain between the Coosa and Tennessee rivers, where Mr. Ferguson found a stone wall "thirty-seven roods and eight feet in length," skirting the brink of a precipice at whose base were five rooms artificially constructed in the solid rock.[2]

One of the the most decisive proofs of the veracity of Bristock's narrative is his assertion that they mummified the corpses of their chiefs previous to interment.

[1] George White, Hist. Colls. of Georgia, p. 423. It has also been described to me by a gentleman resident in the vicinity.

[2] See the Christian Advocate and Journal for 1832, and the almost unintelligible abstract of the article in Josiah Priest's American Antiquities, pp. 169, 170, (third edition, Albany, 1833.) Though the account is undoubtedly exaggerated, it would merit further investigation.

Recent discoveries of such mummies leave us no room to doubt the prevalence of this custom among various Indian tribes east of the Mississippi. It is of so much interest to the antiquarian, that I shall add in an Appendix the details given on this point by later writers, as well as an examination of the origin of those mummies that have been occasionally disinterred in the caves of Tennessee and Kentucky.[1]

One other topic for examination in Bristock's memoir yet remains—the scattered words of the language he mentions. The principal are the following;[2]

Mayrdock—the Viracocha of their traditions.
Naarim—the month of March.
Theomi—proper name of the Gulf of Mexico.
Jauas—priests.
Tlatuici—the mountain tribes.
Paracussi—chief; a generic term.
Bersaykau—vale of cedars.
Akueyas—deer.
Hitanachi—pleasant, beautiful.
Tonatzuli—heavenly singer; the name of a bird sacred to the sun.

Several of these words may be explained from tongues with which we are better acquainted.

Jauas and *Paracussi* are words used in the sense they here bear in many early writers; the derivation of the former will be considered hereafter; that of the latter is uncertain. *Tlatuici* is doubtless identical with *Tsalakie*, the proper appellation of the Cherokee tribe. *Akueyas* has a resemblance, though remote, to

[1] See Appendix II.

[2] I give these according to the orthography of Baumgarten, who may differ slightly from other writers.

the Seminole *ekko* of the same signification. In *hitanachi* we recognize the Choktah intensitive prefix *hhito;* and in *tonatzuli* a compound of the Choktah verb *taloa*, he sings, in one of its forms, with *shutik*, Muskohge *sootah*, heaven or sky. A closer examination would doubtless reveal other analogies, but the above are sufficient to show that these were no mere unmeaning words, coined by a writer's fancy.

The general result of these inquiries, therefore, is strongly in favor of the authenticity of Bristock's narrative. Exaggerated and distorted though it be, nevertheless it is the product of actual observation, and deserves to be classed among our authorities, though as one to be used with the greatest caution. We have also found that though no general migration took place from the continent southward, nor from the islands northward, yet there was considerable intercourse in both directions; that not only the natives of the greater and lesser Antilles and Yucatan, but also numbers of the Guaranay stem of the southern continent, the Caribs proper, crossed the Straits of Florida and founded colonies on the shores of the Gulf of Mexico; that their customs and language became to a certain extent grafted upon those of the earlier possessors of the soil; and to this foreign language the name Apalache belongs. As previously stated, it was used as a generic title, applied to a confederation of many nations at one time under the domination of one chief, whose power probably extended from the Alleghany mountains on the north to the shore of the Gulf; that it included tribes speaking a tongue closely akin to the Choktah is evident from the fragments we have remaining. This is further illustrated by a few words of "Appalachian," preserved by John Chamberlayne.[1] These, with their congeners in cognate dialects, are as follows:

	Apalachian.	*Choktah.*	*Muskohge.*
Father	kelke	aunkky, unky	ilkhy
Heaven	hetucoba	ubbah, *intensitive*, hhito	
Earth	ahan	yahkna	ikahnah
Bread	pasca	puska	

The location of the tribe in after years is very uncertain. Dumont placed them in the northern part of what is now Alabama and Georgia, near the mountains that bear their name. That a portion of them did live in this vicinity is corroborated by the historians of South Carolina, who say that Colonel Moore, in 1703, found them "between the head-waters of the Savannah and Altamaha."[2] De l'Isle, also, locates them between the *R. des Caouitas ou R. de Mai* and the *R. des Chaouanos ou d'Edisco,* both represented as flowing nearly parallel from the mountains.

According to all the Spanish authorities on the other hand, they dwelt in the region of country between the Suwannee and Apalachicola rivers—yet must not be confounded with the Apalachicolos. Thus St. Marks was first named San Marco de Apalache, and it was near here that Narvaez and De Soto found them. They certainly had a large and prosperous town in this vicinity, said to contain a thousand warriors, whose chief was possessed of much influence.[3] De

[1] Oratio Dominica Polyglotta, Amstelædami, 1715. He does not state where he obtained them.

[2] Hewitt, History of South Carolina, Vol. I. p 156.

[3] El Cacique principal de Apalache, Superior de muchos Caciques, Barcia, Ensay. Cron., p. 323.

l'Isle makes this their original locality, inscribing it "*Icy estoient cy devant les Apalaches,*" and their position in his day as one acquired subsequently. That they were driven from the Apalachicola by the Alibamons and other western tribes in 1705, does not admit of a doubt, yet it is equally certain that at the time of the cession of the country to the English, (1763,) they retained a small village near St. Marks, called San Juan.[1] I am inclined to believe that these were different branches of the same confederacy, and the more so as we find a similar discrepancy in the earliest narratives of the French and Spanish explorers.

In the beginning of the eighteenth century they suffered much from the devastations of the English, French, and Creeks; indeed, it has been said, though erroneously, that the last remnant of their tribe "was totally destroyed by the Creeks in 1719."[2] About the time Spain regained possession of the soil, they migrated to the West and settled on the Bayou Rapide of Red River. Here they had a village numbering about fifty souls, and preserved for a time at least their native tongue, though using the French and Mobilian (Chikasah) for common purposes.[3] Breckenridge,[4] who saw them here, describes them as "wretched creatures, who are diminishing daily." Probably by this time the last representative of this once powerful tribe has perished.

[1] Roberts, Hist. of Florida, p. 14.

[2] Schoolcraft's Ind. Tribes, Vol. V. p. 259.

[3] Schermerhorn, Report on the Western Indians in Mass. Hist. Colls. Vol. II. (2 ser.,) p. 26; Alcedo, Hist. and Geog. Dict. of America, Vol. I., p. 82.

[4] Views of Louisiana, p. 150.

CHAPTER III.

PENINSULAR TRIBES OF THE SIXTEENTH CENTURY.

§ 1. SITUATION AND SOCIAL CONDITION.—Caloosas.—Tegesta and Ais.—Tocobaga.—Vitachuco.—Utina.—Soturiba.—Method of Government.
§ 2. CIVILIZATION.—Appearance.—Games.—Agriculture.—Construction of Dwellings.—Clothing.
§ 3. RELIGION.—General Remarks.—Festivals in honor of the Sun and Moon.—Sacrifices.—Priests.—Sepulchral Rites.
§ 4. LANGUAGES.—Timuquana Tongue.—Words preserved by the French.

§ 1.—SITUATION AND SOCIAL CONDITION.

WHEN in the sixteenth century the Europeans began to visit Florida they did not, as is asserted by the excellent bishop of Chiapa, meet with numerous well ordered and civilized nations,[1] but on the contrary found the land sparsedly peopled by a barbarous and quarrelsome race of savages, rent asunder into manifold petty clans, with little peaceful leisure wherein to better their condition, wasting their lives in aimless and unending internecine war. Though we read of the cacique Vitachuco who opposed De Soto with ten thousand chosen warriors, of another who had four thousand always ready for battle,[2] and other such in-

[1] Trovarono terre grandi piene di genti molto ben disposte, savie, politiche, e ben' ordinate. Bartolome de las Casas, Istoria della Distruttione dell' Indie Occidentali, p. 108. Venetia, 1626.
[2] Barcia, Ensay. Cron., p. 71.

stances of distinguished power, we must regard them as the hyperbole of men describing an unknown and strange land, supposed to abound in marvels of every description. The natural laws that regulate the increase of all hunting tribes, the analogy of other nations of equal civilization, the nature of the country, and lastly, the adverse testimony of these same writers, forbid us to entertain any other supposition. Including men, women, and children, the aboriginal population of the whole peninsula probably but little exceeded at any one time ten thousand souls. At the period of discovery these were parcelled out into villages, a number of which, uniting together for self-protection, recognized the authority of one chief. How many there were of these confederacies, or what were the precise limits of each, as they never were stable, so it is impossible to lay down otherwise than in very general terms, dependent as we are for our information on the superficial notices of military explorers, who took an interest in anything rather than the political relations of the nations they were destroying.

Commencing at the south, we find the extremity of the peninsula divided into two independent provinces, one called Tegesta on the shores of the Atlantic, the other and most important on the west or Gulf coast possessed by the Caloosa tribe.

The derivation of the name of the latter is uncertain. The French not distinguishing the final letter wrote it Calos and Callos; the Spaniards, in addition to making the same omission, softened the first vowel till the word sounded like Carlos, which is their usual orthography. This suggested to Barcia and others that the country was so called from the name of its chief, who, hearing from his Spanish captives the grandeur and power of Charles of Spain (Carlos V), in emulation appropriated to himself the title. Doubtless, however, it is a native word; and so Fontanedo, from whom we derive most of our knowledge of the province, and who was acquainted with the language, assures us. He translates it "*village cruel*,"[1] an interpretation that does not enlighten us much, but which may refer to the exercise of the sovereign power. As a proper name, it may be the Muskohge *charlo*, trout, assumed, according to a common custom, by some individual. It is still preserved in the Seminole appellation of the Sanybal river, Carlosa-hatchie and Caloosa-hatchie, and in that of the bay of Carlos, corrupted by the English to Charlotte Harbor, both on the southwestern coast of the peninsula near north latitude 26° 40′.

According to Fontanedo, the province included fifty villages of thirty or forty inhabitants each, as follows: "Tampa, Tomo, Tuchi, Sogo, No which means beloved village, Sinapa, Sinaesta, Metamapo, Sacaspada, Calaobe, Estame, Yagua, Guayu, Guevu, Muspa, Casitoa, Tatesta, Coyovea, Jutun, Tequemapo, Comachica, Quisiyove, and two others; on Lake Mayaimi, Cutespa, Tavaguemme, Tomsobe, Enempa, and twenty others; in the Lucayan Isles, Guarunguve and Cuchiaga." Some of these are plainly Spanish names, while others undoubtedly belong to the native tongue. Of these villages, Tampa has given its name to the inlet formerly called the bay of Espiritu Santo[2] and to the

[1] Memoire, p. 13.

[2] At what time or by whom Tampa Bay was first so called I have not been able to learn. Its usual name in early narratives is Baia de Espiritu Santo, which was given by De Soto; sometimes from separate discoveries it was called

small town at its head. Muspa was the name of a tribe of Indians who till the close of the last century inhabited the shores and islands in and near Boca Grande, where they are located on various old maps. Thence they were driven to the Keys and finally annihilated by the irruptions of the Seminoles and Spaniards.[1] Guaragunve, or Guaragumbe, described by Fontanedo as the largest Indian village on Los Martires, and which means "the village of tears," is probably a modified orthography of Matacumbe and identical with the island of Old Matacumbe, remarkable for the quantity of lignum vitæ there found,[2] and one of the last refuges of the Muspa Indians. Lake Mayaimi, around which so many villages were situated, is identical with lake Okee-chobee, called on the older maps and indeed as late as Tanner's and Carey's, Myaco and Macaco. When Aviles ascended the St. Johns, he was told by the natives that it took its origin "from a great lake called Maimi thirty leagues in extent," from which also streams flowed westerly to Carlos.[3] In sound the word resembles the Seminole *pai-okee* or *pai-hai-o-kee*, grassy lake, the name applied with great fitness by this tribe to the Everglades.[4]

Bahia Honda (Deep Bay,) El Lago de San Bernardo, Baie de St. Louis, and by the Indians Culata (Barcia, Ensayo Cron. p. 342, Torquemada, Monarquia Indiana, Lib. I., Cap. VI.) Herrera in his map of the Audiencia de la Española marks it "B. de tampa," and after him Gerard a Schaagen in the Nov. et Accurat. Americæ Descriptio.

[1] Williams, Hist. of Florida, pp. 36, 212. Ellicott's Journal, p. 247. Robert's Hist. of Florida, p. 17.

[2] Guaicum officinale; the *el palo* or *el palo santo* of the Spaniards.

[3] Barcia, En. Cron. Año 1566.

[4] See Prior's Journal in Williams' Florida, p. 299. The name Miami applied to a tribe in Ohio, and still retained by

When travelling in Florida I found a small body of water near Manatee called lake Mayaco, and on the eastern shore the river Miami preserves the other form of the name.

The chief of the province dwelt in a village twelve or fourteen leagues from the southernmost cape.[1] The earliest of whom we have any account, Sequene by name, ruled about the period of the discovery of the continent. During his reign Indians came from Cuba and Honduras, seeking the fountain of life. He was succeeded by Carlos, first of the name, who in turn was followed by his son Carlos. In the time of the latter, Francesco de Reinoso, under the command of Pedro Menendez de Aviles, the founder of St. Augustine and Adelantado of Florida, established a colony in this territory, which, however, owing to dissensions with the natives, never flourished, and finally the Cacique was put to death by Reinoso for some hostile demonstration. His son was taken by Aviles to Havana to be educated and there baptized Sebastian. Every attempt was made to conciliate him, and reconcile him to the Spanish supremacy but all in vain, as on his return he became "more troublesome and barbarous than ever." This occurred about 1565–1575.[2] Not long after his death the integrity of the state was destroyed, and splitting up into lesser tribes, each lived

two rivers in that State, properly Omaumeg, is said to be a pure Algic word, meaning, People who live on the peninsula. (Amer. Hist. Mag. Vol. III., p. 90.) We are, however, not yet prepared to accept this explanation as applicable to the word as it appears in Florida.

[1] Barcia, Ensay. Cron., p. 49, and compare the Hist. Notable, p. 134.

[2] For these facts see Fontanedo's Memoire, *passim*, and Barcia, Años 1566, 1567.

independent. They gradually diminished in number under the repeated attacks of the Spaniards on the south and their more warlike neighbors on the north. Vast numbers were carried into captivity by both, and at one period the Keys were completely depopulated. The last remnant of the tribe was finally cooped up on Cayo Vaco and Cayo Hueso (Key West), where they became notorious for their inhumanity to the unfortunate mariners wrecked on that dangerous reef. Ultimately, at the cession of Florida, to England in 1763, they migrated in a body to Cuba, to the number of eighty families, since which nothing is known of their fate.[1]

Of the province of Tegesta, situate to the west of the Caloosas, we have but few notices. It embraced a string of villages, the inhabitants of which were famed as expert fishers, (grandes Pescadores,) stretching from Cape Cañaveral to the southern extremity.[2] The more northern portion was in later times called Ais, (Ays, Is) from the native word *aïsa*, deer, and by the Spaniards, who had a post here, Santa Lucea.[3] The residence of the chief was near Cape Cañaveral, probably on Indian river, and not more than five days journey from the chief town of the Caloosas.

At the period of the French settlements, such amity existed between these neighbors, that the ruler of the latter sought in marriage the daughter of Oathcaqua, chief of Tegesta, a maiden of rare and renowned

[1] Bernard Romans, pp. 291–2.

[2] Desde los Martires al Cañaveral, Herrera, Dec. IV., Lib., IV., cap. VII.

[3] Barcia (En. Cron. p. 118) says Ais commences twenty leagues up the St. Johns river; but distances given by the Spanish historians were often mere guesses, quite untrustworthy.

beauty. Her father, well aware how ticklish is the tenure of such a jewel, willingly granted the desire of his ally and friend. Encompassing her about with stalwart warriors, and with maidens not a few for her companions, he started to conduct her to her future spouse. But alas! for the anticipations of love! Near the middle of his route was a lake called Serrope, nigh five leagues about, encircling an island, whereon dwelt a race of men valorous in war and opulent from a traffic in dates, fruits, and a root "so excellent well fitted for bread, that you could not possibly eat better," which formed the staple food of their neighbors for fifteen leagues around. These, fired by the reports of her beauty and the charms of the attendant maidens, waylay the party, rout the warriors, put the old father to flight, and carry off in triumph the princess and her fair escort, with them to share the joys and wonders of their island home.

Such is the romantic story told Laudonniére by a Spaniard long captive among the natives.[1] Why seek to discredit it? May not Serrope be the beautiful Lake Ware in Marion county, which flows around a fertile central isle that lies like an emerald on its placid bosom, still remembered in tradition as the ancient residence of an Indian prince,[2] and where relics of the red man still exist? The dates, *les dattes,* may have been the fruit of the Prunus Chicasaw, an exotic fruit known to have been cultivated by the later Indians, and the bread a preparation of the coonta root or the yam.

North of the province of Carlos, throughout the

[1] Basanier, Hist. Notable, pp. 133–4.
[2] Vignoles, Obs. on the Floridas, pp. 74–5.

country around the Hillsboro river, and from it probably to the Withlacooche, and easterly to the Ocklawaha, all the tribes appear to have been under the domination of one ruler. The historians of De Soto's expedition called the one in power at that period, Paracoxi, Hurripacuxi, and Urribarracuxi, names, however different in orthography, not unlike in sound, and which are doubtless corruptions of one and the same word, otherwise spelled Paracussi, and which was a generic appellation of the chiefs from Maryland to Florida. The town where they found him residing, is variously stated as twenty, twenty-five, and thirty leagues from the coast,[1] and has by later writers been located on the head-waters of the Hillsboro river.[2] In later times the cacique dwelt in a village on Old Tampa Bay, twenty leagues from the main, called Tocobaga or Togabaja,[3] (whence the province derived its name,) and was reputed to be the most potent in Florida. A large mound still seen in the vicinity marks the spot.

This confederacy waged a desultory warfare with their southern neighbors. In 1567, Aviles, then superintending the construction of a fort among the Caloosas, resolved to establish a peace between them, and for this purpose went himself to Tocobaga. He there located a garrison, but the span of its existence was almost as brief as that of the peace he instituted. Subsequently, when the attention of the Spaniards became confined to their settlements on the eastern coast, they lost sight

[1] Biedma, Relation, p. 53; the Port. Gent. in Hackluyt, V., p. 492; La Vega, Lib. II., cap. x., p. 38.

[2] Irving's Conquest of Fla., p. 84, note.

[3] Barcia, Año 1567; Fontanedo, pp. 20, 35.

of this province, and thus no particulars of its after history are preserved.

The powerful chief Vitachuco, who is mentioned in the most extravagant terms by La Vega and the Gentleman of Elvas, seems, in connection with his two brothers, to have ruled over the rolling pine lands and broad fertile savannas now included in Marion and Alachua counties. Though his power is undoubtedly greatly over-estimated by these writers, we have reason to believe, both from existing remains and from the capabilities of the country, that this was the most densely populated portion of the peninsula, and that its possessors enjoyed a degree of civilization superior to that of the majority of their neighbors.

The chief Potavou mentioned in the French accounts, residing about twenty-five leagues, or two days' journey from the territory of Utina, and at war with him, appears to have lived about the same spot, and may have been a successor or subject of the cacique of this province.[1]

The rich hammocks that border the upper St. Johns and the flat pine woods that stretch away on either side of this river, as far south as the latitude of Cape Cañaveral,[2] were at the time of the first settlement of the country under the control of a chief called by the Spanish Utina, and more fully by the French Olata Ouæ Outina. His stationary residence was on the banks of the river near the northern extremity of Lake George, in which locality certain extensive earth-

[1] Basanier, Hist. Notable, pp. 190–1, 108–9, 140 sq.

[2] Jusqu 'à Mayajuaca, dans la contrée de Ais, vers *le lieu planté de roseaux.* Fontanedo, Memoire, p. 35. Cañaveral is a Spanish word signifying the same as the expression I have italicised.

works are still found, probably referable to this period. So wide was his dominion that it was said to embrace more than forty subordinate chiefs,[1] which, however, are to be understood only as the heads of so many single villages. It is remarkable, and not very easy of satisfactory explanation, that among nine of these mentioned by Laudonniére,[2] two, Acquera and Moquoso, are the names of villages among the first encountered by De Soto in his march through the peninsula, and said by all the historians of the expedition to be subject to the chief Paracoxi.

Soturiba (Sotoriva, Satouriona) was a powerful chief, claiming the territory around the mouth of the St. Johns, and northward along the coast nearly as far as the Savannah. Thirty sub-chiefs acknowledged his supremacy, and his influence extended to a considerable distance inland. He showed himself an implacable enemy to the Spaniards, and in 1567, assisted Dominique de Gourgues to destroy their settlements on the St. Johns. His successor, Casicola, is spoken of by Nicolas Bourguignon as the "lord of ten thousand Indians," and ruler of all the land "between St. Augustine and St. Helens."

The political theories on which these confederacies were based, differed singularly in some particulars from those of the Indians of higher latitudes. Among the latter the chief usually won his position by his own valor and wisdom, held it only so long as he maintained this superiority, and dying, could appoint no heir to his pre-eminence. His counsel was sought only in an emergency, and his authority coerced his fellows to no subjection. All this was reversed among

[1] Basanier, Hist. Not. p. 90. [2] Ibid.

the Floridians. The children of the first wife inherited the power and possessions of their father,[1] the eldest getting the lion's share; the sub-chiefs paid to their superior stated tributes of roots, games, skins, and similar articles;[2] and these superiors held unquestioned and absolute power over the persons, property, and time of their subjects.[3] Among the Caloosas, indeed, the king was considered of divine nature, and believed to have the power to grant or withhold seasons favorable to the crops, and fortune in the chase; a superstition the shrewd chief took care to foster by retiring at certain periods almost unattended to a solitary spot, ostensibly to confer with the gods concerning the welfare of the nation.[4] In war the chief led the van with a chosen body guard for his protection,[5] and in peace daily sate in the council house, there both to receive the homage of his inferiors, and to advise with his counsellors on points of national interest. The devotion of the native to their ruler, willingly losing their lives in his defence, is well illustrated in the instance of Vitachuco, killed by De Soto. So scrupulously was the line of demarcation preserved between them and their subjects, that even their food was of different materials.[6]

[1] Basanier, Hist. Not. p. 8.
[2] Hackluyt, Vol. V., p. 492, Fontanedo, p. 15.
[3] Les Floridiens ne sement, ne plantent, ne prennent rien ni à la chasse, ni à la pêche, qui ne soit à la disposition de leurs chefs, qui distribuent, et donnent, comme il leur plait, etc. François Coreal, Voiages, Tome I., p. 44. The chiefs on the Bahamas possessed similar absolute power. (Peter Martyr, De Novo Orbe, Dec. VII., cap. I., p. 467.)
[4] Basanier, Hist. Not., p. 132.
[5] Basanier, pp. 9, 141.
[6] Fontanedo, pp. 10, 11.

§ 2.—Civilization.

The Floridians were physically a large, well proportioned race, of that light shade of brown termed by the French *olivâtre* On the southern coast they were of a darker color, caused by exposure to the rays of the sun while fishing, and are described by Herrera as "of great stature and fearful to look upon," (de grandes cuerpos y de espantosa vista). What rendered their aspect still more formidable to European eyes was the habit of tattooing their skin, practiced for the double purpose of increasing their beauty, and recording their warlike exploits. Though this is a perfectly natural custom, and common wherever a warm climate and public usage permits the uncivilized man to reject clothing a portion of the year, instances are not wanting where it has been made the basis of would-be profound ethnological hypotheses.

In their athletic sports they differed in no notable degree from other tribes. A favorite game was that of ball. In playing this they erected a pole about fifty feet in height in the centre of the public square; on the summit of this was a mark, which the winning party struck with the ball.[1] The very remarkable "pillar" at the Creek town of Atasse on the Tallapoosa river, one day's journey from the Coosa, which puzzled the botanist Bartram,[2] and which a living antiquarian of high reputation has connected with phallic worship,[3] was probably one of these solitary

[1] Basanier, Hist. Not. p. 7.
[2] Travels, p. 456.
[3] E. G. Squier, Aborig. Mon. of N. Y., App. pp. 135–7; Serpent Symbol, pp. 90, 94, 95.

trunks, or else the "red painted great war-pole" of the southern Indians,[1] usually about the same height.

In some parts they had rude musical instruments, drums, and a sort of flute fashioned from the wild cane,[2] the hoarse screeching of which served to testify their joy on festive occasions. A primitive pipe of like construction, the earliest attempt at melody, but producing anything but sounds melodious, was common among the later Chicasaws[3] and the Indians of Central America.[4]

Their agriculture was of that simple character common to most North American tribes. They planted twice in the year, in June or July and March, crops of maize, beans, and other vegetables, working the ground with such indifferent instruments as sticks pointed, or with fish bones and clam-shells adjusted to them.[5] Yet such abundant return rewarded this slight toil that, says De Soto,[6] the largest army could be supported without exhausting the resources of the land. In accordance with their monarchical government the harvests were deposited in public granaries, whence it was dispensed by the chief to every family proportionately to the number of its members. When the stock was exhausted before the succeeding crop was ripe, which was invariably the case, forsaking their fixed abodes, they betook themselves to the woods,

[1] Adair, Hist. N. Am. Inds., p. 205.

[2] They came to meet Narvaez playing on such flutes, "tañendo unas Flautas de Caña," Cabeza de Vaca, Naufragios, cap. V.

[3] Bernard Romans, p. 62.

[4] Francisco Ximenez, Origen de los Indios de Guatemala, p. 179.

[5] De Morgues, Brevis Historia, Tab. XXI.

[6] Lettre écrite par l'Adelantade Soto, etc., p. 46.

where an abundance of game, quantities of fish and oysters, and the many esculent vegetables indigenous in that latitude, offered them an easy and not precarious subsistence.

Their dwellings were collected into a village, circular in form, and surrounded with posts twice the height of a man, set firmly in the ground, with interfolding entrance. If we may rely on the sketches of De Morgues, taken from memory, the houses were all round and the floors level with the ground, except that of the chief, which occupied the centre of the village, was in shape an oblong parallelogram, and the floor somewhat depressed below the surface level.[1] In other parts the house for the ruler and his immediate attendants was built on an elevation either furnished by nature or else artificially constructed. Such was the "hie mount made with hands," described by the Portuguese Gentleman at the spot where De Soto landed, and which is supposed by some to be the one still seen in the village of Tampa. Some of these were of sufficient size to accommodate twenty dwellings, with roads leading to the summits on one side, and quite inaccessible on all others.

Most of the houses were mere sheds or log huts thatched with the leaf of the palmetto, a plant subservient to almost as many purposes as the bread-fruit tree of the South Sea Islands. Occasionally, however, the whole of a village was comprised in a single enormous habitation, circular in form, from fifty to one hundred feet in diameter. Into its central area, which was sometimes only partially roofed, opened numerous

[1] Brevis Historia, Tab. XXX., and compare the Histoire Memorable, p. 261.

cabins, from eight to twelve feet square, arranged around the circumference, each the abode of a separate family. Such was the edifice seen by Cabeza de Vaca "that could contain more than three hundred persons" (que cabrian mas de trecientas personas);[1] such that found by De Soto in the town of Ochile on the frontiers of the province of Vitachuco; such those on the north-eastern coast of the peninsula described by Jonathan Dickinson.[2]

The agreeable temperature that prevails in those latitudes throughout the year did away with much of the need of clothing, and consequently their simple wardrobe seems to have included nothing beyond deerskins dressed and colored with vegetable dyes, and a light garment made of the long Spanish moss (*Tillandsia usneoides*), the gloomy drapery of the cypress swamps, or of the leaves of the palmetto. A century and a half later Captain Nairn describes them with little or no clothing, "all painted," and with no arms but spears, "harpoos," pointed with fish bones.

§ 3.—Religion.

It is usual to consider the religion and mythology of a nation of weighty import in determining its origin; but to him, who regards these as the spontaneous growth of the human mind, brought into existence by the powers of nature, nourished by the mental constitution of man, and shaped by external

[1] Naufragios, cap. III.

[2] God's Protecting Providence, p. 62. This style of building was common among the Caribs, and may have been derived from them.

circumstances, all of which are "everywhere different yet everywhere the same," general similarities of creed and of rite appear but deceptive bases for ethnological theories. The same great natural forces are eternally at work, above, around and beneath us, producing similar results in matter, educing like conceptions in mind. He who attentively compares any two mythologies whatever, will find so many points of identity and resemblance that he will readily appreciate the capital error of those who deduce original unity of race from natural conformity of rite. Such is the fallacy of those who would derive the ancient population of the American continent from a fragment of an insignificant Semitic tribe in Syria; and of the Catholic missionaries, who imputed variously to St. Thomas and to Satan the many religious ceremonies and legends, closely allied to those of their own faith, found among the Aztecs and Guatemalans.

In investigations of this nature, therefore, we must critically distinguish between the local and the universal elements of religions. Do we aim by analysis to arrive at the primal theistic notions of the human mind and their earliest outward expression? The latter alone can lead us. Or is it our object to use mythology only as a handmaid to history, an index of migrations, and a record of external influence? The impressions of local circumstances are our only guides.

The tribes of the New World, like other early and uncivilized nations, chose the sun as the object of their adoration; either holding it to be itself the Deity, as did most of the indwellers of the warm zones, or, as the natives of colder climes, only the most august object of His creation, a noble emblem of Himself. Intimately connected with both, ever recurring in some one of its Protean forms, is the worship of the reciprocal principle.

The Floridian Indians belonged to the first of these classes. They worshipped the sun and moon, and in their honor held such simple festivals as are common in the earlier stages of religious development. Among these the following are worthy of specification.

After a successful foray they elevated the scalps of their enemies on poles decked with garlands, and for three days and three nights danced and sang around them.[1] The wreaths here probably had the same symbolical significance as those which adorned the Athenian Hermes,[2] or which the Maypures of the Orinoco used at their weddings, or those with which the northern tribes ornamented rough blocks of stone.

Their principal festival was at the first corn-planting, about the beginning of March. At this ceremony a deer was sacrificed to the sun, and its body, or according to others its skin stuffed with fruits and grain, was elevated on a tall pole or tree stripped of its branches, an object of religious veneration, and around which were danced and sung the sacred choruses;[3] a custom also found by Loskiel among the Delawares,[4] and which, recognizing the deer or stag as a solar emblem, surmounting the phallic symbol, the upright stake, has its parallel in Peruvian heliolatry and classical mythology.

The feast of Toya, though seen by the French north

[1] Basanier, Hist. Not., pp. 8, 101.

[2] See Mackay, Progress of the Intellect, Vol. II., p. 143, note 152, and authorities there quoted.

[3] Brevis Historia, Tab. XXXV.; Baumgarten, Geschichte von Amerika, B. I., s. 87.

[4] Klemm, Culturgeschichte der Menscheit, B. II, s. 179.

of the peninsula and perhaps peculiar to the tribes there situate, presents some remarkable peculiarities. It occurred about the end of May, probably when the green corn became eatable. Those who desired to take part in it, having apparelled themselves in various attire, assembled on the appointed day in the council house. Here three priests took charge of them, and led them to the great square, which they danced around thrice, yelling and beating drums. Suddenly at a given signal from the priests they broke away "like unbridled horses" (commechevaux débridez), plunging into the thickest forests. Here they remained three days without touching food or drink, engaged in the performance of mysterious duties. Meanwhile the women of the tribe, weeping and groaning, bewailed them as if dead, tearing their hair and cutting themselves and their daughters with sharp stones; as the blood flowed from these frightful gashes, they caught it on their fingers, and, crying out loudly three times *he Toya*, threw it into the air. At the expiration of the third day the men returned; all was joy again; they embraced their friends as though back from a long journey; a dance was held on the public square; and all did famous justice to a bounteous repast spread in readiness.[1] The analogy that these rites bear to the Διονυσια and similar observances of the ancients is very striking, and doubtless they had a like significance. The singular predominance of the number three, which we shall also find repeated in other connections, cannot escape the most cursory reader. Nor is this a rare or exceptional instance where it occurs in American religions; it is

[1] Basanier, Hist. Not., pp. 43 sqq.

bound up in the most sacred myths and holiest observances all over the continent.[1] Obscure though the reason may be, certain it is that the numbers three, four, and seven, are hallowed by their intimate connection with the most occult rites and profoundest mysteries of every religion of the globe, and not less so in America than in the older continent.

In the worship of the moon, which in all mythologies represents the female principle, their rites were curious and instructive. Of those celebrated at full moon by the tribes on the eastern coast, Dickinson, an eye-witness, has left us the following description :—"The moon being up, an Indian who performeth their ceremonies, stood out, looking full at the moon, making a hideous noise and crying out, acting like a mad-man for the space of half an hour, all the Indians being silent till he had done; after which they all made a fearful noise, some like the barking of a dogg or wolf, and other strange sounds; after this one gets a logg and setts himself down; holding the stick or logg upright on the ground, and several others getting about him, made a hideous noise, singing to our amazement." This they kept up till midnight, the women taking part.[2]

On the day of new moon they placed upright in the ground "a staff almost eight foot long having a broad arrow on the end thereof, and thence half-way painted red and white, like unto a barber's-pole; in the middle of the staff is fixed a piece of wood like unto the thigh, legg, and foot of a man, and the lower part thereof is

[1] On the Trinity in aboriginal American religions, see Count Stolberg in the Wiener Yahrbücher der Literatur, B. XVI., s. 278.

[2] God's Protecting Providence, p. 12.

painted black." At its base was placed a basket containing six rattles; each taking one and making a violent noise, the six chief men of the village including the priest danced and sang around the pole till they were fatigued, when others, painted in various devices, took their place; and so on in turn. These festivities continued three days, the day being devoted to rest and feasting, the night to the dance and fasting; during which time no woman must look upon them.[1] How distinctly we recognize in this the worship of the reciprocal principle!—that ever novel mystery of reproduction shadowed forth by a thousand ingenious emblems, by a myriad strange devices, all replete with a deep significance to him who is versed in the subtleties of symbolism. Even among these wretched savages we find the colors black, white, and red, retain that solemn import so usual in oriental mythi.

The representation of a leg used in this observance must not be considered a sign of idolatry, for, though the assertion, advanced, by both Adair[2] and Klemm,[3] that no idols whatever were worshipped by the hunting tribes, is unquestionably erroneous and can be disproved by numerous examples, in the peninsula of Florida they seem to have been totally unknown. The image of a bird, made of wood, seen at the village where De Soto first landed, cannot be regarded as such, but was

[1] God's Protecting Providence, pp. 38, 39.

[2] Hist. of the North Am. Indians, p. 22. He embraces all tribes "from Hudson Bay to the Mississippi," and adds that they had no lascivious or Priapean images or rites, in which he is equally at fault.

[3] Man hat weder bei den Sudamericanern noch bei den Nördlichen eigentliche G ö t z e n b i l d e r oder I d o l e bemerkt. Culturgeschichte der Menschheit, B. II., s. 172. This is confined of course to the "Yägervolker."

a symbol common among several of the southern tribes, and does not appear to have had any special religious meaning.

Human sacrifice, so rare among the Algic nations, was not unknown, though carried to by no means such an appalling extent as among the native accolents of the Mississippi. The chief of the Caloosas immolated every year one person, usually a Christian, to the principle of evil (al Demonio)[1], as a propitiary offering; hence on one old map, that of De L'Isle, they are marked "Les Carlos Antropophages." Likewise around the St. Johns they were accustomed to sacrifice the first-born son, killing him by blows on the head;[2] but it is probable this only obtained to a limited observance. In all other cases their offerings consisted of grains and fruits.

The veneration of the serpent, which forms such an integral part of all nature religions, and relics of which are retained in the most perfected, is reported to have prevailed among these tribes. When a soldier of De Gourgues had killed one, the natives cut off its head and carried it away with great care and respect (avec vn grand soin et diligence).[3] The same superstitious fear of injuring these reptiles was retained in later days by the Seminoles.[4]

The priests constituted an important class in the community. Their generic appellation, *javas, jauas,*

[1] Barcia, Ensayo Cron. Año 1566, p. 94; the Port. Gent. in Hackluyt, Vol. V. p. 491, mentions this as existing among the tribes near Tampa Bay.

[2] Moris apud illos est primogenitum masculum Regi victimum offerre, etc. Brevis Historia, Tab. XXXIV.

[3] La Reprinse de la Floride, p. 264.

[4] Wm. Bartram, Travels, p. 263, and compare Adair, Hist. of the North Am. Inds. pp. 238–9.

jaruars, jaovas, jaonas, jaiias, javiinas,—for all these and more orthographies are given—has been properly derived by Adair from the meaningless exclamation *yah-wah*, used as name, interjection, and invocation by the southern Indians. It is not, however, an etymon borrowed from the Hebrew as he and Boudinot argue, but consists of two slightly varied enunciations of the first and simplest vowel sound; as such, it constitutes the natural utterance of the infant in its earliest wail, and, as the easiest cry of relief of the frantic devotee all over the world, is the principal constituent of the proper name of the deity in many languages. Like the medas of the Algonquins and the medicine men of other tribes, they united in themselves the priest, the physician, and the sorcerer. In sickness they were always ready with their bag of herbs and simples, and so much above contempt was their skill in the healing art that not unfrequently they worked cures of a certain troublesome disease sadly prevalent among the Indians and said by some to have originated from them. Magicians were they of such admirable subtlety as to restore what was lost, command the unwilling rain from heaven in time of drought, and foretell the position of an enemy or the result of a battle. As priests, they led and ordered festivals, took part in grave deliberations, and did their therapeutic art fail to cure, were ready with spiritual power to console, in the emergencies of pain and death.

Their sepulchral rites were various. Along the St. Johns, when a chief died they interred the corpse with appropriate honors, raised a mound two or three feet high above the grave, surrounded it with arrows fixed in the ground, and on its summit deposited the conch, *le hanap*, from which he was accustomed to drink. The tribe fasted and mourned three days and three nights, and for six moons women were employed to bewail his death, lamenting loudly thrice each day at sunrise, at mid-day, and at sunset.[1] All his possessions were placed in his dwelling, and the whole burnt; a custom arising from a superstitious fear of misfortune consequent on using the chattels of the dead, a sentiment natural to the unphilosophic mind. It might not be extravagant to suppose that the shell had the same significance as the urn so frequent in the tombs of Egypt and the sepulchres of Magna Græcia, "an emblem of the hope that should cheer the dwellings of the dead."[2] The burial of the priests was like that of the chiefs, except that the spot chosen was in their own houses, and the whole burnt over them, resembling in this a practice universal among the Caribs, and reappearing among the Natchez, Cherokees and Arkansas, (Taencas).

Among the Caloosas and probably various other tribes, the corpses were placed in the open air, apparently for the purpose of obtaining the bones when the flesh had sufficiently decomposed, which, like the more northern tribes, they interred in common sepulchres, heaping dirt over them so as to form mounds. It was as a guard to watch over these exposed bodies, and to prevent their desecration by wild beasts, that Juan Ortiz, the Spaniard of Seville, liberated by De Soto, had been employed while a prisoner among the nations of the Gulf Coast.

[1] Brevis Historia, Tab. XL. Basanier, Hist. Not., pp. 10, 11.
[2] Mackay, Progress of the Intellect, Vol. II., p. 129.

§ 4.—Language.

A philological examination of the Floridian tribes, which would throw so much light on their origin, affiliation, and many side-questions of general interest, must for the present remain unattempted, save in a very inadequate manner. Not but that there exists material, ample and well-arranged material, but it is not yet within reach. I have already spoken of the works of the Father Pareja, the learned and laborious Franciscan, and of the good service he did the missionaries by his works on the Timuquana tongue. Not a single copy of any of these exists in the United States, and till a republication puts them within reach of the linguist, little can be done towards clearing up the doubt that now hangs over the philology of this portion of our country. What few extracts are given by Hervas, hardly warrant a guess as to their classification.

The name Timuquana, otherwise spelled Timuaca, Timagoa, and Timuqua, in which we recognize the Thimogona of the French colonists, was applied to the tongue prevalent in the immediate vicinity of St. Augustine and toward the mouth of the St. Johns. It was also held in estimation as a noble and general language, a sort of *lingua franca,* throughout the peninsula. Pareja remarks, "Those Indians that differ most in words and are roughest in their enunciation (mas toscos), namely those of Tucururu[1] and of Santa

[1] Tucururu or Tacatacuru was on the Atlantic coast south of St. Augustine, between it and Santa Lucea. (Barcia, En. Cron., p. 121.)

Lucea de Acuera, in order to be understood by the natives of the southern coast, who speak another tongue, use the dialect of Moscama, which is the most polished of all (la mas politica), and that of Timuquana, as I myself have proved, for they understood me when I preached to them."[1]

This language is remarkable for its singularly numerous changes in the common names of individuals, dependent on mutual relationship and the varying circumstances of life, which, though not the only instance of the kind in American tongues, is here extraordinarily developed, and in the opinion of Adelung seems to hint at some previous, more cultivated condition (in gewissen Hinsicht einen cultivirteren Zustand des Volks anzeigen möchte).[2] For example, *iti*, father, was used only during his life; if he left descendants he was spoken of as *siki*, but if he died without issue, as *naribica-pasano*: the father called his son *chirico-viro*, other males *kie*, and all females *ulena*. Such variations in dialect, or rather quite different dialects in the same family, extraordinary as it may seem to the civilized man, were not very uncommon among the warlike, erratic hordes of America. They are attributable to various causes. The esoteric language of the priests of Peru and Virginia might have been either meaningless incantations, as those that of yore resounded around the Pythian and Delphic shrines, or the *disjecta membra* of some ancient tongue, like the Dionysiac songs of Athens. When as among the Abipones of Paraguay, the Natchez of Louisiana, and the Incas of

[1] Hervas, Catalogo de las Lenguas de las naciones conocidas, Tom. I. p. 387. Madrid, 1800–1805.

[2] Mithridates, oder Allgemeine Sprachenkunde, B. III., s. 285.

Peru, the noble or dominant race has its own peculiar tongue, we must impute it to foreign invasion, and a subsequent rigorous definition of the line of cast and prevention of amalgamation. Another consequence of war occurs when the women and children of the defeated race are alone spared, especially should the males be much absent and separated from the females; then each sex has its peculiar language, which may be preserved for generations; such was found to be the case on some of the Caribbee islands and on the coast of Guiana. Also certa insuperstitious observances, the avoidance of evil omens, and the mere will of individuals, not seldom worked changes of this nature. In such cases these dialects stand as waymarks in the course of time, referring us back to some period of unity, of strife, or of migration, whence they proceeded, and as such, require the greatest caution to be exercised in deducing from them any general ethnographical inferences.

What we are to judge in the present instance is not yet easy to say. Hervas does not hesitate to assert that abundant proof exists to ally this with the Guaranay (Carib) stock. Besides a likeness in some etymons, he takes pains to lay before the reader certain similar rites of intermarriage, quotes Barcia to show that Carib colonies actually did land on Florida, and adds an ideal sketch of the *Antigua configuracion del golfo Mexicano y del mar Atlantico,* thereon proving how readily in ancient ages, under altered geological conditions, such a migration could have been effected.

Without altogether differing from the learned abbé in his position, for it savors strongly of truth, it might be well, with what material we have at hand, to see whether other analogies could be discovered.

The pronominal adjectives and the first three numerals are as follows;—

na	mine	mile	our
ye	thine	yaye	your
mima	his	lama	their
	minecotamano	one	
	naiuchanima	two	
	nakapumima	three	

Now, bearing in mind that the pronouns of the first and second persons and the numerals are primitive words, and that in American philology it is a rule almost without exception that personal pronouns and pronominal adjectives are identical in their consonants,[1] we have five primitive words before us. On comparing them with other aboriginal tongues, the *n* of the first person singular is found common to the Algonquin Lenape family, but in all other points they are such contrasts that this must pass for an accidental similarity. A resemblance may be detected between the Uchee *nowah*, two, *nokah*, three, and *naiucha*-mima, *naka*-pumima. Taken together, *iti-na*, my father, sounds not unlike the Cherokee *etawta*, and Adelung notices the slight difference there is between *niha*, eldest brother, and the Illinois *nika*, my brother. But these are trifling compared to the affinities to the Carib, and I should not be astonished if a comparison of Pareja with Gilü and D'Orbigny placed beyond doubt its relationship to this family of languages. Should this brief notice give rise to such an investigation, my object in inserting it will have been accomplished.

The French voyagers occasionally noted down a

[1] Gallatin, Trans. Am. Antiq. Soc., Vol. II., p. 178.

word or two of the tongues they encountered, and indeed Laudonniére assures us that he could understand the greater part of what they said. Such were *tapagu tapola*, little baskets of corn, *sieroa pira*, red metal, *antipola bonnasson*, a term of welcome meaning, brother, friend, or something of that sort (qui vaut autant à dire comme frère, amy, ou chose semblable).[1] Albert Gallatin[2] subjected these to a critical examination, but deciphered none except the last. This he derives from the Choktah *itapola*, allies, literally, they help each other, while "in Muskohgee, *inhisse*, is, his friends, and *ponhisse*, our friends," which seems a satisfactory solution. It was used as a friendly greeting both at the mouth of the St. Johns and thirty leagues north of that river; but this does not necessarily prove the natives of those localities belonged to the Chahta family, as an expression of this sort would naturally gain wide prevalence among very diverse tribes.

Fontanedo has also preserved some words of the more southern languages, but none of much importance.

[1] Basanier, Hist. Not. pp. 67, 69, 72; Coppie d'une Lettre venant de la Floride, p. 244.

[2] Trans. Am. Antiq. Soc., Vol. II., p. 106.

CHAPTER IV.

LATER TRIBES.

§ 1. Yemassees.—Uchees.—Apalachicolos.—Migrations northward.
§ 2. Seminoles.

§ 1.—YEMASSEES AND OTHER TRIBES.

ABOUT the close of the seventeenth century, when the tribes who originally possessed the peninsula had become dismembered and reduced by prolonged conflicts with the whites and between themselves, various bands from the more northern regions, driven from their ancestral homes partly by the English and partly by a spirit of restlessness, sought to fix their habitations in various parts of Florida.

The earliest of these were the Savannahs or Yemassees (Yammassees, Jamasees, Eamuses,) a branch of the Muskogeh or Creek nation, who originally inhabited the shores of the Savannah river and the low country of Carolina. Here they generally maintained friendly relations with the Spanish, who at one period established missions among them, until the arrival of the English. These purchased their land, won their friendship, and embittered them against their former friends. As the colony extended, they gradually migrated southward, obtaining a home by wresting from their red and white possessors the islands and mainland along the coast of Georgia and Florida. The most disastrous of these inroads was in 1686, when they drove the Spanish colonists from all the islands north of the St. Johns, and laid waste the missions and plantations that had been commenced upon them. Subsequently, spreading over the savannas of Alachua and the fertile plains of Middle Florida, they conjoined with the fragments of older nations to form separate tribes, as the Chias, Canaake, Tomocos or Atimucas, and others. Of these the last-mentioned were the most important. They dwelt between the St. Johns and the Suwannee, and possessed the towns of Jurlo Noca, Alachua, Nuvoalla, and others. At the devastation of their settlements by the English and Creeks in 1704, 1705 and 1706, they removed to the shores of Musquito Lagoon, sixty-five miles south of St. Augustine, where they had a village, long known as the Pueblo de Atimucas.

A portion of the tribe remained in Carolina, dwelling on Port Royal Island, whence they made frequent attacks on the Christian Indians of Florida, carrying them into captivity, and selling them to the English. In April, 1715, however, instigated as was supposed by the Spanish, they made a sudden attack on the neighboring settlements, but were repulsed and driven from the country. They hastened to St. Augustine, "where they were received with bells ringing and guns firing,"[1] and given a spot of ground within a mile of the city. Here they resided till the attack of Colonel Palmer in 1727, who burnt their village and destroyed most of its inhabitants. Some, however, escaped, and to the number of twenty men, lived in St. Augustine about the middle of the century. Finally, this last miserable

[1] Hewitt, Hist. of S. Car., Vol. I., p. 222. He gives 1714 as the date of this occurrence. But see Carroll's Hist. Colls. of S. Car., Vol. II., p. 353.

remnant was enslaved by the Seminoles, and sunk in the Ocklawaha branch of that tribe.[1]

Originating from near the same spot as the Yemassees were the Uchees. When first encountered by the whites, they possessed the country on the Carolina side of the Savannah river for more than one hundred and fifty miles, commencing sixty miles from its mouth, and, consequently, just west of the Yemassees. Closely associated with them here, were the Palachoclas or Apalachicolos. About the year 1716, nearly all the latter, together with a portion of the Uchees, removed to the south under the guidance of Cherokee Leechee, their chief, and located on the banks of the stream called by the English the Flint river, but which subsequently received the name of Apalachicola.

The rest of the Uchees clung tenaciously to their ancestral seats in spite of the threats and persuasion of the English, till after the middle of the century, when a second and complete migration took place. Instead of joining their kinsmen, however, they kept more to the east, occupying sites first on the headwaters of the Altamaha, then on the Santilla, (St. Tillis,) St. Marys, and St. Johns, where we hear of them as early as 1786. At the cession to the United States, (1821,) they had a village ten miles south of Volusia, near Spring Gardens. At this period, though intermarrying with their neighbors, they still maintained their identity, and when, at the close of the Seminole war in 1845, two hundred and fifty Indians

[1] On the Yemassees consult Hewitt, ubi suprà; Barcia, En. Cron. Año 1686; the tracts in Carroll's Hist. Colls. of S. Car., Vol. II., pp. 106, 246, 353, 355; Roberts, Hist. of Florida, p. 15; Notices of E. Florida, by a recent traveller, p. 57.

embarked at Tampa for New Orleans and the West, it is said a number of them belonged to this tribe, and probably constituted the last of the race.[1]

Both on the Apalachicola and Savannah rivers this tribe was remarkable for its unusually agricultural and civilized habits, though of a tricky and dishonest character. Bartram[2] gives the following description of their town of Chata on the Chatauchee:—"It is the most compact and best situated Indian town I ever saw; the habitations are large and neatly built; the walls of the houses are constructed of a wooden frame, then lathed and plastered inside and out, with a redish, well-tempered clay or mortar, which gives them the appearance of red brick walls, and these houses are neatly covered or roofed with cypress bark or shingles of that tree." This, together with the Savanuca town on the Tallapoosa or Oakfuske river, comprised the whole of the tribe at that time resident in this vicinity.

Their language was called the Savanuca tongue, from the town of that name. It was peculiar to themselves and radically different from the Creek tongue or Lingo, by which they were surrounded; "It seems," says Bartram, "to be a more northern tongue;" by which he probably means it sounded harsher to the ear. It was said to be a dialect of the Shawanese, but a comparison of the vocabularies indicates no connection, and

[1] On the migrations of this tribe consult the Colls. of the Georgia Hist. Soc. Vol. I., pp. 145–6; Vol. II., pp. 61, 71; John Filson; The Disc., Settlement, and Pres. State of Kentucké, App. 3, p. 84; Gallatin in Trans. Am. Antiq. Soc., Vol. II., pp. 84, 95; Notices of E. Fla., by a recent traveller, p. 59; Narrative of Oceola Nikkanoche, p. 70 et seq.; Moll's Map of the Northern Parts of America, and Sprague's Hist. of the Florida War.

[2] Travels, pp. 388–9, and see p. 486.

it appears more probable that it stands quite alone in the philology of that part of the continent.

While these movements were taking place from the north toward the south, there were also others in a contrary direction. One of the principal of these occurred while Francisco de la Guerra was Governor-General of Florida, (1684–1690,) in consequence of an attempt made by Don Juan Marquez to remove the natives to the West India islands and enslave them. We have no certain knowledge how extensive it was, though it seems to have left quite a number of missions deserted.[1]

What has excited more general attention is the tradition of the Shawnees, (Shawanees, Sawannees, Shawanos,) that they originally came from the Suwannee river in Florida, whose name has been said to be "a corruption of Shawanese," and that they were driven thence by the Cherokees.[2] That such was the origin of the name is quite false, as its present appellation is merely a corruption of the Spanish *San Juan*, the river having been called the Little San Juan, in contradistinction to the St. Johns, (el rio de San Juan,) on the eastern coast.[3] Nor did they ever live in this region, but were scions of the Savannah stem of the Creeks, accolents of the river of that name, and consequently were kinsmen of the Yemassees.

[1] Barcia, Ensayo Cronologico, Año 1686, p. 287.

[2] Jedediah Morse, Rep. on Ind. Affairs, App. p. 93, Archæol- Amer., Vol. I., p. 273, and others.

[3] Other forms of the same are Little St. Johns, Little Savanna, Seguano, Suannee, Swannee. It was also called the Carolinian river.

§ 2.—The Seminoles.

The Creek nation, so called says Adair from the number of streams that intersected the lowlands they inhabited, more properly Muskogeh, (corrupted into Muscows,) sometimes Western Indians, as they were supposed to have come later than the Uchees,[1] and on the early maps Cowetas (Couitias,) and Allibamons from their chief towns, was the last of those waves of migration which poured across the Mississippi for several centuries prior to Columbus. Their hunting grounds at one period embraced a vast extent of country reaching from the Atlantic coast almost to the Mississippi. After the settlement of the English among them, they diminished very rapidly from various causes, principally wars and the ravages of the small-pox, till about 1740 the whole number of their warriors did not exceed fifteen hundred. The majority of these belonged to that branch of the nation, called from its more southern position the Lower Creeks, of mongrel origin, made up of the fragments of numerous reduced and broken tribes, dwelling north and north-west of the Floridian peninsula.[2]

When Govenor Moore of South Carolina made his attack on St. Augustine, he included in his complement a considerable band of this nation. After he had been

[1] H. R. Schoolcraft, Notes on the Iroquois, p. 161. Adair, however, says they recorded themselves to be *terræ filii.* (Hist. N. Am. Inds., p. 257, but compare p. 195.)

[2] For the individual nations composing the confederacy see Romans, Hist. of Fla., p. 90; Roberts, Hist. of Fla., p. 13, and Adair, p. 257.

repulsed they kept possession of all the land north of the St. Johns, and, uniting with certain negroes from the English and Spanish colonies, formed the nucleus of the nation, subsequently called *Ishti semoli*, wild men,[1] corrupted into Seminolies and Seminoles, who subsequently possessed themselves of the whole peninsula and still remain there. Others were introduced by the English in their subsequent invasions, by Governor Moore, by Col. Palmer, and by General Oglethorpe. As early as 1732, they had founded the town of Coweta on the Flint river, and laid claim to all the country from there to St. Augustine.[2] They soon began to make incursions independent of the whites, as that led by Toonahowi in 1741, as that which in 1750, under the guidance of Secoffee, forsook the banks of the Apalachicola, and settled the fertile savannas of Alachua, and as the band that in 1808 followed Micco Hadjo to the vicinity of Tallahassie. They divided themselves into seven independent bands, the Latchivue or Latchione, inhabiting the level banks of the St. Johns, and the sand hills to the west, near the ancient fort Poppa, (San Francisco de Pappa,) opposite Picolati, the Oklevuaha, or Oklewaha on the river that bears their name, the Chokechatti, the Pyaklekaha, the Talehouyana or Fatehennyaha, the Topkelake, and a seventh, whose name I cannot find.

According to a writer in 1791,[3] they lived in a state

[1] Giddings (Exiles of Florida, p. 3) gives the incorrect translation "runaways," and adds, "it was originally used in reference to the Exiles long before the Seminole Indians separated from the Creeks." The Upper Creeks called them Aulochawan. (American State Papers, Vol. V., p. 813.)

[2] Establishment of the Colony of Georgia, pp. 10, 12, in Peter Force's Historical Tracts, Vol. I.

[3] Major C. Swan, in Schoolcraft's Hist. of the Indian Tribes. Vol. V., pp. 260, 272.

of frightful barbarity and indigence, and were "poor and miserable beyond description." When the mother was burdened with too many children, she hesitated not to strangle the new-born infant, without remorse for her cruelty or odium among her companions. This is the only instance that I have ever met in the history of the American Indians where infanticide was in vogue for these reasons, and it gives us a fearfully low idea of the social and moral condition of those induced by indolence to resort to it. Yet other and by far the majority of writers give us a very different opinion, assure us that they built comfortable houses of logs, made a good, well-baked article of pottery, raised plenteous crops of corn, beans, pumpkins, sweet potatoes, tobacco, swamp and upland rice, peas, melons and squashes, while in an emergency the potatoe-like roots of the china brier or red coonta, the tap root of the white coonta,[1] the not unpleasant cabbage of the palma royal and palmetto, and the abundant game and fish, would keep at a distance all real want.[2]

As may readily be supposed from their vagrant and unsettled mode of life, their religious ideas were very simple. Their notion of a God was vague and ill-defined; they celebrated certain festivals at corn planting and harvest; they had a superstition regarding the transmigration of souls and for this purpose held the infant over the face of the dying mother;[3]

[1] *Smilax*, *China*, and *Zamia pumila.*

[2] On the civilization of the Seminoles, consult Wm. Bartram, Travels, pp. 192–3, 304, the American Jour. of Science, Vol. IX., pp. 133, 135, and XXXV., pp. 58–9; Notices of E. Fla ,by a recent Traveller, and the works on the Florida War.

[3] Narrative of Oceola Nikkanoche, p. 75. The author supposed this was to receive the injunctions of the dying mother, but more probably it sprang from that belief in a *metasoma-*

and from their great reluctance to divulge their real names, it is probable they believed in a personal guardian spirit, through fear of offending whom a like hesitation prevailed among other Indian tribes, as well as among the ancient Romans, and, strange to say, is in force to this day among the lower class of Italians.[1] They usually interred the dead, and carefully concealed the grave for fear it should be plundered and desecrated by enemies, though at other times, as after a battle, they piled the slain indiscriminately together, and heaped over them a mound of earth. One instance is recorded[2] where a female slave of a deceased princess was decapitated on her tomb to be her companion and servant on the journey to the land of the dead.

A comparison of the Seminole with the Muskogeh vocabulary affords a most instructive lesson to the philologist. With such rapidity did the former undergo a vital change that as early as 1791 "it was hardly understood by the Upper Creeks."[3] The later changes are still more marked and can be readily

tosis which prevailed, and produced analogous customs in other tribes. See La Hontan, Voiages, Tome I, p. 232; "Brebeuf, Relation de la Nouv. France pour l'an 1636, ch. IX." Pedro de Cieza, Travs. in Peru, ch. XXXII., p. 86 in Steven's Collection.

[1] Notices of East Fla., by a recent traveller, p. 79. For the extent and meaning of this singular superstition, see Schoolcraft, Oneota, pp. 331, 456; Algic Researches, Vol. I., p. 149, note; Hist. of the Indian Tribes, Vol. III., p. 66; Gregg, Commerce of the Prairies, Vol. II., p. 271; Bradford, American Antiquities, p. 415; Mackay, Progress of the Intellect, Vol. I., p. 146, and note [15].

[2] Narrative of Oceola Nikkanoche, p. 77.

[3] C. Swan in Schoolcraft's His. Ind. Tribes, Vol. V., p. 260.

studied as we have quite a number of vocabularies preserved by different writers.

Ever since the first settlement of these Indians in Florida they have been engaged in a strife with the whites,[1] sometimes desultory and partial, but usually bitter, general, and barbarous beyond precedent in the bloody annals of border warfare. In the unanimous judgment of unprejudiced writers, the whites have ever been in the wrong, have ever enraged the Indians by wanton and unprovoked outrages, but they have likewise ever been the superior and victorious party. The particulars of these contests have formed the subjects of separate histories by able writers, and consequently do not form a part of the present work.

Without attempting a more minute specification, it will be sufficient to point out the swift and steady decrease of this and associated tribes by a tabular arrangement of such censual statistics as appear most worthy of trust.

[1] By the whites I refer to the descendants of the English of the northern states. While under the Spanish government, up to the first Seminole war, their nation was said to be "numerous, proud and wealthy." (Vignoles, Obs. on the Floridas, App., p. 215.) This was owing to the Spanish laws which gave them equal privileges with white and free colored persons, and drew the important distinction that they could hold land *individually*, but not *nationally*. How different these beneficent regulations from the decree of the Florida Legislature in 1827, that any male Indian found out of the reservation "shall receive not exceeding thirty-nine stripes on his bare back, and his gun be taken away from him." (Laws relating to Inds. and Ind. Affairs, p. 247, Washington, 1832,) and similar enactments.

Censual Statistics of the Lower Creeks and Seminoles.

Date.	*Number.*	*Authority.*	*Remarks.*
1716	1000	Roberts[1]	L. Creek war. on Flint river.
1734	1350	Anon.[2]	Lower Creek warriors.
1740	1000	Anon.[3]	" " "
1774	2000	Wm. Bartram[4]	Lower Creeks.
1776	3500	Romans[5]	Gun-men of U. and L. Creeks.
1820	1200	Morse[6]	"Pure blooded Seminoles."
1821	5000	J. H. Bell[7]	All tribes in the State.
1822	3891	Gad Humphreys[8]	Seminoles E. of Apalachicola
1823	4883	Pub. Docs.[9]	All tribes in the State.
1836	1660	Sprague[10]	Serviceable warriors.
1843	42	Sprague[11]	Pure Seminole warriors.
1846	70	Sprague[12]	" " "
1850	70	Sprague[13]	" " "
1856	150	Pub. papers	Mixed warriors.
1858	80	Pub. papers	" "

Probably within the present year (1859) the last of this nation, the only free representatives of those many tribes east of the Mississippi that two centuries since held undisturbed sway, will bid an eternal farewell to their ancient abodes, and leave them to the quiet possession of that race that seems destined to supplant them.

[1] Roberts, First Disc. of Fla., p. 90.
[2] Collections of Georgia Hist. Soc. Vol. II., p. 318.
[3] Ibid., p. 73.
[4] Travels, p. 211.
[5] Nat. History, p. 91.
[6] Report on Indian Affairs, p. 33.
[7] Cohen, Notices of Florida, p. 48.
[8] Sprague, Hist. of the Fla. War, p. 19.
[9] American State Papers, Vol. VI., p. 439.
[10] Hist. of the Fla. War, p. 97.
[11] Ibid., p. 409.
[12] Ibid., p 512.
[13] Ibid.

CHAPTER V.

THE SPANISH MISSIONS.

Early Attempts.—Efforts of Aviles.—Later Missions.—Extent during the most flourishing period.—Decay.

It was ever the characteristic of the Spanish conqueror that first in his thoughts and aims was the extension of the religion in which he was born and bred. The complete history of the Romish Church in America would embrace the whole conquest and settlement of those portions held originally by France and Spain. The earliest and most energetic explorers of the New and much of the Old World have been the pious priests and lay brethren of this religion. While others sought gold they labored for souls, and in all the perils and sufferings of long journeys and tedious voyages cheerfully bore a part, well rewarded by one convert or a single baptism. With the same zeal that distinguished them everywhere else did they labor in the unfruitful vineyard of Florida, and as the story of their endeavors is inseparably bound up with the condition of the natives and progress of the Spanish arms, it is with peculiar fitness that the noble toils of these self-denying men become the theme of our investigation.

The earliest explorers, De Leon, Narvaez, and De Soto, took pains to have with them devout priests as well as bold lancers, and remembered, which cannot be said of all their cotemporaries, that though the natives might possess gold, they were not devoid of souls. The latter included in his complement no less than twelve priests, eight lay brethren, and four clergymen of inferior rank; but their endeavors seem to have achieved only a very paltry and transient success.

The first wholly missionary voyage to the coast of Florida, and indeed to any part of America north of Mexico, was undertaken by Luis Cancel de Balbastro, a Dominican friar, who in 1547 petitioned Charles I. of Spain to fit out an armament for converting the heathen of that country. A gracious ear was lent to his proposal, and two years afterwards, in the spring of 1549, a vessel set sail from the port of Vera Cruz in Mexico, commanded by the skillful pilot Juan de Arana, and bearing to their pious duty Luis Cancel with three other equally zealous brethren, Juan Garcia, Diego de Tolosa, and Gregorio Beteta. Their story is brief and sad. Going by way of Havana they first struck the western coast of the peninsula about 28° north latitude the day after Ascension day. After two months wasted in fruitless efforts to conciliate the natives in various parts, when all but Beteta had fallen martyrs to their devotion to the cause of Christianity, the vessel put back from her bootless voyage, and returned to Vera Cruz.[1]

Some years afterwards (1559), when Don Tristan de Luna y Arellano founded the colony of Santa Maria

[1] Relation de la Floride apportée par Frère Gregorio de Beteta, in Ternaux's *Recueil*. They did not touch the coast beyond the Bay of Apalache nor much south of Tampa Bay. Both Barcia (En. Cron. Año 1549) and Herrera (Dec. VIII., Lib. V., cap. XIV., XV.) say they entered the latter, but this cannot be, as the supposed description is entirely inapplicable. For other particulars see Eden's translation of Peter Martyr, (fol. 319, Londini, 1555.)

de Felipina near where Pensacola was subsequently built, he was accompanied by a provincial bishop and a considerable corps of priests, but as his attempt was unsuccessful and his colony soon disbanded, they could have made no impression on the natives.[1]

It was not till the establishment of a permanent garrison at St. Augustine by the Adelantado Pedro Menendez de Aviles, that the Catholic religion took firm root in Floridian soil. In the terms of his outfit is enumerated the enrollment of four Jesuit priests and twelve lay brethren. Everywhere he displayed the utmost energy in the cause of religion; wherever he placed a garrison, there was also a spiritual father stationed. In 1567 he sent the two learned and zealous missionaries Rogel and Villareal to the Caloosas, among whom a settlement had already been formed under Francesço de Reinoso. At their suggestion a seminary for the more complete instruction of youthful converts was established at Havana, to which among others the son of the head chief was sent, with what success we have previously seen.

The following year ten other missionaries arrived, one of whom, Jean Babtista Segura, had been appointed Vice Provincial. The majority of these worked with small profit in the southern provinces, but Padre Antonio Sedeño settled in the island of Guale,[2] and is to be remembered as the first who drew up a grammar and catechism of any aboriginal tongue north of

[1] The authority for this, as well as most of the facts in this chapter where other references are not given, is Barcia's Ensayo Cronologico.

[2] Sometimes called Santa Maria or St. Marys; now Amelia Island, so named, from the beauty of its shores, by Gov. Oglethorpe in 1736. (Francis Moore, Voyage to Georgia, in Ga. Hist. Soc.'s Colls. Vol. I., p. 124)

Mexico; but he reaped a sparse harvest from his toil; for though five others labored with him, we hear of only seven conversions, and four of these infants *in articulo mortis.* Yet it is also stated that as early as 1566 the Adelantado himself had brought about the conversion of these Indians *en masse.* A drought of eight months had reduced them to the verge of starvation. By his advice a large cross was erected and public prayer held. A tremendous storm shortly set in, proving abundantly to the savages the truth of his teachings. But they seem to have turned afresh to their wallowing in the mire.

In 1569, the Padre Rogel gave up in despair the still more intractable Caloosas; and among the more cultivated nations surrounding San Felipe, north of the Savannah river, sought a happier field for his efforts. In six months he had learned the language and at first flattered himself much on their aptness for religious instruction. But in the fall, when the acorns ripened, all his converts hastened to decamp, leaving the good father alone in his church. And though he followed them untiringly into woods and swamps, yet "with incredible wickedness they would learn nothing, nor listen to his exhortations, but rather ridiculed them, jeopardizing daily more and more their salvation." With infinite pains he collected some few into a village, gave them many gifts, and furnished them food and mattocks; but again they most ungratefully deserted him "with no other motive than their natural laziness and fickleness." Finding his best efforts thrown away on such stiff-necked heathen, with a heavy heart he tore down his house and church, and, shaking the dust off his feet, quitted the country entirely.

At this period the Spanish settlements consisted of three colonies: St. Augustine, originally built south of where it now stands on St. Nicholas creek, and changed in 1566, San Matteo at the mouth of the river of the same name, now the St. Johns,[1] and fifty leagues north of this San Felipe in the province of Orista or Santa Helena, now South Carolina. In addition to these there were five block-houses, (casas fuertes), two, Tocobaga and Carlos, on the western coast, one at its southern extremity, Tegesta, one in the province of Ais or Santa Lucea, and a fifth, which Juan Pardo had founded one hundred and fifty leagues inland at the foot of certain lofty mountains, where a cacique Coava ruled the large province Axacàn.[2] There seem also to have been several minor settlements on the St. Johns.

Such was the flourishing condition of the country when that "terrible heretic and runaway galley slave," as the Spanish chronicler calls him, Dominique de Gourgues of Mont Marsain, aided by Pierre le Breu, who had escaped the massacre of the French in 1565, and the potent chief Soturiba, demolished the most important posts (1567). Writers have over-rated the injury this foray did the colony. In reality it served but to stimulate the indomitable energy of Aviles. Though he himself was at the court of Spain and obliged to remain there, with the greatest promptness he dispatched Estevan de las Alas with two hundred

[1] Called by the natives Ylacco or Walaka, the river of many lakes; by the French Rivière Mai, as Ribaut entered it on the first of that month; by the Spaniards Rio Matheo, Rio Picolato, on some charts by mistake Rio San Augustin, Rio Matanca and Rio Caouita, and not till much later Rio San Juan, which the English changed to St. Johns, and St. Whan.

[2] Barcia, p. 123, and cf., p. 128.

and seventy-three men, who rebuilt and equipped San Matheo, and with one hundred and fifty of his force quartered himself in San Felipe.

With him had gone out quite a number of priests. The majority of these set out for the province of Axacàn, under the guidance of the brother of its chief, who had been taken by Aviles to Spain, and there baptized, in honor of the viceroy of New Spain, Don Luis de Velasco. His conversion, however, was only simulation, as no sooner did he see the company entirely remote from assistance, than, with the aid of some other natives, he butchered them all, except one boy, who escaped and returned to San Felipe. Three years after (1569), the Adelantado made an attempt to revenge this murder, but the perpetrators escaped him.

Notwithstanding these drawbacks, at the time of the death of Aviles, a firm and extensive foundation had been laid for the Christian religion, though it was by no means professed, as has been asserted, "by all the tribes from Santa Helena, on the north, to Boca Rattones, on the south, and from the Atlantic to the Gulf of Mexico."[1]

After his death, under the rule of his nephew, Pedro Menendez Marquez, a bold soldier but a poor politician, the colony seems to have dwindled to a very insignificant point. Spanish historians speak vaguely of many nations reduced by him, but such accounts cannot be trusted. At the time of the destruction of St. Augustine by Drake, in 1586, this town was built of wood, and garrisoned by one hundred and fifty men.[2] And

[1] Williams, Florida, p. 175.

[2] Though Drake left nothing but the fort, and the dwellings were a second time destroyed by Col. Palmer, in 1727, yet Stoddard. (Sketches of Louisiana, p. 120) says houses were standing in his time bearing the date 1571 !

if we may believe the assertions of the prisoners he brought to England, the whole number of souls, both at this place and at Santa Helena, did not exceed two hundred.[1] Only six priests were in the colony; and as to the disposition of the Indians, it was so hostile and dangerous, that for some time subsequent the soldiers dared never leave the fort, even to hunt or fish.[2] Yet it was just about this time (1584), that Williams,[3] on the authority of his ancient manuscript, states that "the Spanish authorities were acknowledged as far west as the river Mississippi (Empalazada), and north one hundred and forty leagues to the mountains of Georgia!"

As early as 1566, fourteen women had been introduced by Sancho de Arminiega; but we read of no increase, and it is probable that for a long series of years the colony was mainly supported by fresh arrivals.

It was not till 1592, when, in pursuance of an ordinance of the Council of the Indies, twelve Franciscans were deputed to the territory, that the missions took a new start. They were immediately forwarded to various quarters of the province, and for a while seem to have been quite successful in their labors. It is said that in 1594 there were "no less than twenty mission houses." One of these priests, Pedro de Corpa, superior of the mission of Tolemato (Tolemaro) near the mouth of the St. Marys river, by his unsparing and harsh rebukes, excited the anger of the natives to such a degree that,

[1] Hackluyt, Vol. III., p. 432. Pedro Morales adds, "The greatest number of Spanyards that have beene in Florida these sixe yeeres, was 300."

[2] Torquemada, Monarquia Indiana, Lib. XIX., cap. XX., p. 350.

[3] Nat. and Civ. Hist. of Fla., p. 175.

headed by the chief of Guale, they rose *en masse*, and murdered him at the foot of the altar. Nor did this glut their vengeance. Bearing his dissevered head upon a pole as a trophy and a standard, they crossed to the neighboring island of Guale, and there laid waste the missions Topiqui, Asao, Ospo, and Assopo. The governor of St. Augustine lost no time in hastening to the aid of the sufferers; and, though the perpetrators of the deeds could nowhere be found, by the destruction of their store-houses and grain fields, succeeded by a long drought, "which God visited upon them for their barbarity," such a dreadful famine fell upon them that their tribe was nearly annihilated (1600).

In 1602, Juan Altimirano, bishop of Cuba, visited this portion of his diocess, and was much disheartened by the hopeless barbarity of the natives.. So much so, indeed, that years afterwards, when holding discussion with the bishop of Guatemala concerning the query, "Is God known by the light of Nature?" and the latter pressing him cogently with Cicero, he retorted, "Ah, but Cicero had not visited Florida, or he would never have spoken thus."

This discouraging anecdote to the contrary, the very next year, in the general assembly that met at Toledo, Florida, in conjunction with Havana and Bahama, was constituted a Custodia of eleven convents, and in 1612, they were elevated into an independent Provincia, under the name of Santa Helena, with the head convent at Havana, and Juan Capillas appointed first Provincial Bishop.[1] An addition of thirty-two Franciscans, partly under Geronimo de Ore in 1612, and partly sent out

[1] Torquemada, Monarquia Indiana, Lib. XIX., cap. XX., p. 350; Barcia, Años 1603 and 1612.

by Philip III., the year after, sped the work of conversion, and for a long time subsequent, we find vague mention of nations baptized and churches erected.

About the middle of the century, (1649,) the priests had increased to fifty, and the episcopal revenue amounted to four hundred dollars. At this time St. Augustine numbered "more than three hundred inhabitants." So great had been the success of the spiritual fathers, that in 1655, Diego de Rebolledo, then Governor and Captain-General, petitioned the king to erect the colony into a bishopric; a request which, though favorably viewed, was lost through delay and procrastination. Similar attempts, which were similarly frustrated, were made by hissuccessors Juan Marquez in 1682, and Juan Ferro in 1689.

Notwithstanding these indications of a lively energy, a very different story is told by the traveller of Carthagena, Francois Coreal, who visited the peninsula in 1669. He mentions no settlements but San Augustine and San Matheo,—indeed, expressly states that there were none,[1]—and even these were in a sorry plight enough, (assez degarnies.) Either he must have been misinformed, or the work of conversion proceeded with great and sudden rapidity after his visit, as less than twenty years afterwards, (1687,) when by the attempts of Juan Marquez to remove the natives to the West India Islands, many forsook their homes for distant regions, they left a number of missions deserted, as San Felipe, San Simon, Sapola, Obaldiqui, and others. This marked increase was largely owing to a subsidy of twenty-four Franciscans under Alonzo

[1] L'interieur, non plus que les parties de l'ouest et du Nord n'est pas en notre pouvoir. Voiages aux Indes Occidentales, T. I., p. 27.

de Moral in 1676, and the energetic action of the Bishop of Cuba, who spared no pains to facilitate the advent of missionaries to all parts.[1]

In pursuance of the advice of Pablo de Hita, Governor-General, attempts were renewed in 1679 to convert the nations of the southern extremity of the peninsula, and in 1698, there were fourteen Franciscans employed among them. These Indians are described as "idolaters and given to all abominable vices," and not a few of the missionaries suffered martyrdom in their efforts to reclaim them.[2]

Towards the close of the century, (1696,) the condition of St. Augustine is described by Jonathan Dickinson[3] as follows:—"It is about three-quarters of a mile in length, not regularly built, the houses not very thick, they having large orchards, in which are plenty of *oranges, lemmons, pome-citrons, lymes, figgs,* and *peaches:* the houses, most of them, are old buildings, and not half of them inhabited. The number of men that belong to government being about three hundred, and many of them are kept as sentinalls at their lookouts. At the north end of the town stands a large fortification, being a quadrangel with bastions. Each bastion will contain thirteen guns, but there is not passing two-thirds of fifty-two mounted. . . . The wall of the fortification is about thirty foot high, built of sandstone sawed [coquina rock]. . . . . The fort is moated round."

The colony of Pensacola or Santa Maria de Galve,

[1] He published two Cedulas Reales for this purpose, bearing the dates Oct. 20, 1680, and Sept. 30, 1687.

[2] Barcia, p. 317; Careri, Voyage round the World, in Churchill's Coll., Vol. IV., p. 537.

[3] God's Protecting Providence, pp. 77–8.

founded by Andres de Pes in 1693, gradually increasing in importance and maintaining an overland connection with St. Augustine, naturally gave rise to intermediate settlements, for which the fertile, wide-spread savannas of Alachua, the rich hammocks along the Suwannee, and the productive limestone soil of Middle Florida offered unrivalled advantages.

The tractable Apalaches and their neighbors received the missionaries with much favor, and it is said that almost all the former were converted;[1] a statement which we must confine, however, to that small portion of the confederated tribes included under this title, that lived in Middle Florida. When Colonel Moore invaded their country in 1703–4, he found them living in villages, each having its parish church, subsisting principally by agriculture, and protected by a garrison of Spanish soldiers.[2] The open well-cleared character of their country, and the marks of their civilized condition were long recalled in tradition by the later Indians.[3] So strong a hold did Catholicism take upon them that more than a century subsequent, when the nation was reduced to an insignificant family on the Bayou Rapide, they still retained its forms, corrupted by admixture with their ancient heliolatry.[4]

On the Atlantic coast, there were besides St. Augustine the towns of San Matheo, Santa Cruce, San Juan,

[1] Maintenant ils sont presquetouts Chrètiens. Louys Morery, Le Grand Dictionnaire Historique, ou le Melange Curieux, Vol. I., Art. *Apalaches.* (Amsterdam and La Haye, 1702.)

[2] See the Report on Oglethorpe's Expedition, and Col. Moore's Letter to the Governor, in Carroll's Hist. Colls. of S. C., Vol. II.

[3] Williams, View of W. Fla., p. 107.

[4] Alcedo, Dict. of America, Vol. I., p. 81.

Santa Maria, and others. The Indians of these missions Dickinson[1] describes as scrupulous in their observance of the Catholic rites, industrious and prosperous in their worldly relations, "having plenty of hogs and fowls, and large crops of corn;" and each hamlet presided over by "Fryars," who gave regular instruction to the native children in school-houses built for the purpose. All these were north of St. Augustine; to the south the savages were more perverse, and in spite of the earnest labors of many pious priests, some of whom fell martyrs to their zeal, they clung tenaciously to heathendom.

Nothing definite is known regarding the settlements on and near the Gulf, but in all probability they were more extensive than those on the eastern shore, peopling the coast and inland plains with a race of civilized and Christian Indians. Cotemporary geographers speak of "the towns of Achalaque, Ossachile, Hirritiqua, Coluna, and some others of less note,"[2] as founded and governed by Spaniards, while numerous churches and villages are designated on ancient charts, with whose size and history we are totally unacquainted. Many of these doubtless refer to native hamlets, while the Spanish names affixed to others point to settlements made by that nation. How much the Church of Rome had at heart the extension and well-being of this portion of her domain, may be judged from the fact that she herself bore half the expense of the military kept in the province for its protection.[3]

Such was the condition of the Spanish missions of

[1] God's Protecting Providence, pp. 68–9.

[2] Herman Moll, Thesaurus Geographus, Pt. II, p. 211, 4th ed. London, 1722.

[3] Dickinson, God's Protecting Prov., p. 63.

Florida at their most flourishing period. Shortly after the commencement of the eighteenth century, foes from the north destroyed and drove out the colonists, demolishing in a few years all that the life, and the blood, and the toil of so many martyrs during two centuries had availed to construct. About the middle of the century we have a tolerably accurate knowledge of the country through English writers; and then so few and insignificant were the Spanish settlements, that only one occurred between St. Marks and St. Augustine, while, besides the latter, the only post on the Atlantic coast was a wretched "hut" on the south bank of the St. Johns at its mouth.[1]

Undoubtedly it is to the close of the seventeenth century therefore that we must refer those vestiges of an extensive and early inhabitation that occasionally meet our notice in various parts. Sometimes in the depth of forests of apparently primeval growth the traveller has been astonished to find rusting church bells, half buried brass cannon, mouldering walls, and the decaying ruins of once stately edifices. Especially numerous are these in middle Florida, along the old Spanish highway from St. Augustine to Pensacola, on the banks of the St. Johns, and on Amelia island. The Indians informed the younger Bartram[2] that near the Suwannee, a few miles above Manatee Spring, the Spaniards formerly had "a rich, well cultivated, and populous settlement, and a strong fortified post, as they likewise had at the savanna and field of Capola," east of the Suwannee, between it and the Alachua plains; but that these were far inferior to those on the Apala-

[1] Roberts, Hist. of Fla., p. 15, and Francis Moore's Voyage to Georgia.

[2] Travels, p. 233.

chian Old Fields "where yet remain vast works and buildings, fortifications, temples, &c." The elder Bartram[1] speaks of similar remarkable antiquities on the St. Johns, Bernard Romans[2] in various parts of the interior, Williams,[3] Brackenridge,[4] and others[5] in middle Florida, and I may add the numerous Spanish Old Fields which I observed throughout the peninsula, the extensive coquina quarries on Anastasia (St. Estaca, Fish's) Island, and the deserted plantations on Musquito and Indian river Lagoons, as unequivocal proofs of a much denser population than is usually supposed to have existed in those regions.

The easy conquest these settlements offered to the English and the rapidity with which they melted away were partly owing to the insufficient force kept for their protection. Colonel Daniels, who led the land force of Governor Moore's army in 1702, and took possession of St. Augustine, apparently met with no noticeable opposition on his march; while we have it on official authority that the year after there were only three hundred and fifty-three soldiers in the whole province of whom forty-five were in Apalache, seven in Timuqua, nineteen in Guale, and the rest in St. Augustine.

The incursion of the English in 1702–1706, and of the Creeks (Alibamons) in 1705, were very destructive

[1] Travels in E. Fla., p. 32, Darlington, Mems. of Bartram and Marshall, p, 284.

[2] Nat. Hist. E. and W. Fla , pp. 277–8.

[3] Nat. and Civil Hist. Fla. Preface and p. 175.

[4] See his letter on the Antiquities of the State in Williams' View of W. Fla., pp. 105–110.

[5] The War in Fla., by a late Staff Officer, p. 5; see also, the account of Black Hoof in Morse's Rep. on Ind. Affairs, App. p. 98, and cf. Archæol. Am., Vol. I. p. 273.

to the monastic establishments of the north, and though Juan de Ayala, minister of the interior, devoted himself earnestly to restoring them, his labor was destined to yield small profit. The destruction of Pensacola by Bienville in 1719, the ravages of Colonel Palmer eight years later, the second demolition of the settlements in Apalache, between Tallahassie and St. Marks, by a marauding party of English and Indians in 1736, the inroad of Governor Oglethorpe four years subsequent, and another incursion of the English in 1745—these following in quick succession, it may be readily conceived rendered of no avail the efforts of the Franciscans to re-establish their missions on Floridian soil.

Previous to the cession to England the settlements had become reduced to St. Josephs, Pensacola, and St. Marks on the Gulf, Picolati on the St. Johns, and St. Augustine on the Atlantic. When the English took possession, the latter town numbered nine hundred houses and five thousand seven hundred inhabitants including a garrison of two thousand five hundred men.[1] There was a well-built church here as also at Pensacola, while at St. Marks there were two convents, one of Jesuits the other of Franciscans.[2] At this time but very few of the Indians, who are described as "bigotted idolators worshipping the sun and moon," and "noted for a bold, subtile, and deceitful people,"[3] seem to have been in the fold of the Catholic Church.

Harassed and worn out as the colony was by long wars, and apparently soon to die a natural death, it is

[1] Dr. Stork, Des. of E. Fla., p. 8.
[2] Capt. Robinson, in Roberts, p. 97.
[3] Roberts, Hist. of Fla, p. 5.

not a matter of wonder that in the tripartite Definitive Treaty of Peace signed at Versailles, February 10th, 1763, Spain was glad to relinquish her right to its soil in consideration of the far superior island of Cuba.[1] Though it was stipulated that all who desired to remain should enjoy their property-rights, and religion, very few availed themselves of the privilege, little loth to forsake a country that had been one continued scene of war and tumult for more than half a century.

With this closes the history of the conversion of the Indians as during the English regime they were lost sight of in other issues, and when the Spanish returned to power such a scene of unquiet turmoil and ceaseless wrangling awaited them as effectually to divert their attention from the moral condition of the aboriginal tribes.

[1] Parliamentary History, Vol. XV., Col. 1301, Art. XX.

CHAPTER VI.

ANTIQUITIES.

Mounds.—Roads.—Shell Heaps.—Old Fields.

THE descriptions left by the elder and younger Bartram of the magnitude and character of the Floridian antiquities, had impressed me with a high opinion of their perfection, and induced large expectations of the light they might throw on the civilization of the aborigines of the peninsula; but a personal examination has convinced me that they differ little from those common in other parts of our country, and are capable of a similar explanation. Chief among them are the mounds. These are not infrequent upon the rich lowlands that border the rivers and lakes; and so invariably did their builders choose this position, that during the long journeys I made in the prairies and flat pine woods east of the St. Johns as well as over the rolling and fertile country between this river and the Gulf, as far south as Manatee, I never saw one otherwise located. An enumeration and description of some of the most noteworthy will suffice to indicate their character and origin.

On Amelia island, some half a mile east of Fernandina new town, there is an open field, containing some thirty acres, in shape an isosceles triangle, clothed with long grass and briary vines, bounded on all sides by dense thickets of myrtle, live-oak, palmetto, yellow pine and cedar. About midway of the base of this triangle, stands a mound thrown up on the extremity of a natural ridge, which causes its height to vary from twenty to five-and-thirty feet on the different sides. It is composed of the common surface sand, obtained from the east side, close to the base, where an excavation is visible. A few live-oaks and pines grow upon it, the largest of which, at the time of my visit (1856), measured seventeen inches in diameter. There is a fine view from the summit, embracing on the west the vast marshes between Amelia island and the mainland, with a part of St. Mary's sound, across which, northward, lie the woody shores of Cumberland island, projected in dark relief against the glittering surf of the Atlantic, which stretches away in a brilliant white line to the north-east, loosing itself in the broad expanse of ocean that bounds the eastern horizon. Hence, one of its uses was, doubtless, as a look-out or watch-tower; but from excavations, made by myself and others, it proved, like every similar mound I examined, or heard of as examined, in Florida, to be, in construction, a vast tomb. Human bones, stone axes, darts, and household utensils, were disinterred in abundance. Quantities of rudely marked fragments of pottery, and broken oyster, clam, and conch shells, were strewed over the field. I was informed of a second mound, smaller in size, somewhat south of Fernandina light-house; but owing to the brevity of my stay, and the incredible swarms of musquitoes that at that season infested the woods, I did not visit it. I could learn nothing of the two large tumuli on this island, known as the "Ogeechee Mounts," mentioned by the younger Bartram.[1]

On Fleming's Island, at the mouth of Black Creek,

[1] Travels, p. 65.

identified by Sparks with the "extremely beautiful, fertile, and thickly inhabited" Edelano of the French colonists, and on Murphy's Island, eight miles above Pilatka, are found mounds of moderate size, and various other vestiges of their ancient owners. But far more remarkable than these are the large constructions on the shores and islands at the southern extremity of Lake George, first visited and described as follows, by John Bartram,[1] in 1766: "About noon we landed at Mount Royal, and went to see an Indian tumulus, which was about one hundred yards in diameter, nearly round, and twenty foot high. Found some bones scattered on it. It must be very ancient, as live-oak are growing upon it three foot in diameter; directly south from the tumulus is an avenue, all the surface of which has been taken off and thrown on one side, which makes a bank of about a rood wide and a foot high, more or less, as the unevenness of the ground required, for the avenue is as level as a floor from bank to bank, and continues so for three quarters of a mile, to a pond of water about one hundred yards wide and one hundred and fifty long, north and south,—seemed to be an oblong square, and its banks four foot perpendicular, gradually sloping every way to the water, the depth of which we do not say, but do not imagine it deep, as the grass grows all over it; by its regularity it seems to be artificial; if so, perhaps the sand was carried from thence to raise the tumulus."

A description of this mound is also given by Wm. Bartram, who visited it both with his father, and fifteen years later.[2] In summing up the antiquities, he saw in Florida, this author says,[3] "from the river

[1] Jour. of Travels in E. Fla., p. 25.
[2] Travels, p. 99. [3] Ibid., p. 521.

St. Juans southerly to the point of the peninsula of Florida are to be seen high pyramidal mounts with spacious and extensive avenues leading from them out of the town to an artificial lake or pond of water. The great mounts, highways, and artificial lakes up St. Juans on the east shore, just at the entrance of the great Lake George; one on the opposite shore, on the bank of the Little lake, another on Dunn's island, a little below Charlotteville, and one on the large beautiful island just without the Capes of Lake George, in sight of Mount Royal, and a spacious one on the West banks of Musquitoe river near New Smyrna, are the most remarkable of this sort that occurred to me."

The artificial lakes in this account are the excavations made in obtaining material, since filled with water. The highways, which, in another passage, the above quoted writer describes as "about fifty yards wide, sunk a little below the common level, and the earth thrown up on each side, making a bank of about two feet high,"[1] seem, from both French and Spanish accounts to have been not unusual among the natives. Laudonniére mentions one of great beauty that extended from the village of Edelano to the river some three hundred paces in length,[2] and another still more considerable at the head quarters of the powerful chief Utina,[3] which must have been very near if not identical with that at Mount Royal. La Vega, in his

[1] Travels, p. 99.

[2] Au sorty du village d'Edelano, pour venir au port de la rivière il faut passer par une allée, longue environ de trois cens pas et large de quinze, aux deux costez de laquelle sont plantez de grands arbres, &c. Hist. Notable, p. 138.

[3] Il y a au sortir du village une grande allée de trois à quatre cens pas, laquelle et recouverte de grands arbres des deux costez. Hist. Not., pp. 164–5.

remarkable chapter on the construction of the native villages,[1] speaks of such broad passages leading from the public square at the base to the house of the chief on the summit of the mound that the natives were accustomed to throw up for its site. What we are to understand by the royal highways, *Caminos Reales*, near Tampa Bay, that lead from one town to another, (que van de un Pueblo al otro,)[2] an expression that would not be applicable to mere trails, is not very evident.

Six miles by water above Lake Monroe, near the shore of a small lagoon on the left bank of the river, stands an oval mound of surface soil filled with human bones of so great an age, and so entirely decomposed, that the instrument with which I was digging passed through them with as much ease as through the circumjacent earth. Yet, among these ancient skeletons, I discovered numerous small blue and large white glass beads, undoubtedly inhumed at the formation of the tumulus. The bodies were all of adults and no special order in their deposition seemed to have been observed. Previous to my visit, I was informed that small earthenware articles had been disinterred, some of which were simply pyramids of triangular bases, whose use had much puzzled the finder. We know that this form, sacred in the mythologies of the old world to the worship of the productive power, had also a strong religious significance among the Natchez, and many other aboriginal tribes,[3] and probably in connection with the burial of the dead, it possessed among the Floridians,

[1] Conq. de la Florida, Lib. II., P. I , cap. ult.

[2] La Vega, Ibid., Lib. I., cap. V., pp. 30–1.

[3] Lafitau in Baumgarten, Geschichte von Amerika, B. I., s. 71; Schoolcraft, Algic Researches, Vol. II., pp. 52, 190.

as it did among the ancients and orientals,[1] a symbolical connection with the immortality of the soul and the life after death.

In the rich hammock half a mile below Lake Harney on the left bank of the St. Johns, is a large oval mound, its transverse diameter at base forty yards, and thirty feet in height. It is surrounded by a ditch whence the soil of which it is constructed was taken. An extremely luxuriant vegetation covers the whole hammock and the mound itself, though few of the trees indicate a great age. On the same side of the river twenty miles above the lake, is another similar mound. They are abundant on the rich lands of Marion and Alachua counties, and in the hammocks of the Suwannee, and are found at least as far south as Charlotte's Harbor and the Miami river. There is one on the government reserve in Tampa, another at the head of Old Tampa Bay, and a third on Long Key, Sarasota Bay. A portion of the latter has been washed away by the waters of the gulf and vast numbers of skeletons exposed, some of which I was assured by an intelligent gentleman of Manatee, who had repeatedly visited the spot and examined the remains, were of astonishing size and must have belonged to men seven or eight feet in height. This statement is not so incredible as it may appear at first sight. Various authors report instances of equally gigantic stature among the aborigines of our country. The chiefs of the province of Chicora, a portion of what is now South Carolina, were famous for their height, which was supposed to

[1] Knight, Anc. Art. sect. 162; Mackay, Progress of the Intellect, Vol. I., p. 198, note [28]; Montfaucon, Antiquities, Vol. II, p. 235; Görres, Mythengeschichte, B. I., s. 171.

prove their royal blood;[1] some inhabitants of the province of Amichel on the Gulf of Mexico were not less remarkable in this respect;[2] and Beverly found among certain human bones religiously preserved in a temple of the Virginian Indians an *os femoris*, measuring two feet nine inches in length;[3] while in our own days, Schoolcraft saw a humerus at Fort Hill, New York,[4] and Lanman, sundry bones in a cave in Virginia[5] that must have belonged to men compared to whom ours is but a race of dwarfs.

On the opposite banks of Silver Spring run, respectively a quarter of a mile and a mile and a half below the head, there are two tumuli. Pottery, axes, and arrow-heads abound in the vicinity, and every sign goes to show that this remarkable spot was once the site of a populous aboriginal settlement.

What now are the characteristics of this class of Floridian mounds? In summing up the whole available knowledge respecting them, we arrive at the conclusion that to whatever purpose they may have subsequently been applied, they were originally constructed as vast cemeteries. Mount Royal tumulus is but a heap of bones covered with earth, and none have as yet been opened but disclosed the same contents. They are very simple in construction. I saw

[1] Real Cedula que contiene el asiento capitulado con Lucas Vasquez de Aillon, in Navarrete Viages, Tom. III. p. 153; Basanier, Hist. Notable, p. 29, and comp., p. 78.

[2] Real cedula dando facultad à Francisco de Garay para poblar la Provincia de Amichel, in Navarrete, Tom. III., p. 148. The account says they were "de diez à once palmos en alto."

[3] Histoire de la Virginie, Liv. III., p. 259, (Orleans, 1707.)

[4] Notes on the Iroquois, p. 482.

[5] Letters from the Allegheny Mountains, Let. XX. p. 162.

no well-defined terraces, no groups of mounds, none with rectangular or octagonal bases, no ditches but those made in excavating material, no covered ways, no stratification; in short, none of those signs of a comparatively advanced art that distinguish the earthworks of Ohio. Their age is not great. Some indeed are covered with trees of large size, and in one case the annual rings were said to count back to the year 1145,[1] (a statement, however, that needs confirmation,) but the rapid growth of vegetation in that latitude requires but a few years to produce a forest. The plantation of Lord Rolles, deserted some fourscore years since, is now overgrown with pines a foot in diameter, and I have seen old fields still bearing the marks of cultivation covered with lofty forests, and a spot of cleared land, forsaken for ten years, clothed with a thriving growth of palmetto and oak. Moreover, savage and civilized, all men agree in leaving nature to adorn the resting places of the dead, and hence it is an egregious error to date the passing away of a nation from the oldest tree we find on its graves. Rather, when we recollect that from the St. Lawrence to the Pampas, many tribes did religious homage to certain trees, and when we remember how universal a symbol they are of birth and resurrection, should we be surprised were they not cultivated and fostered on the sepulchres of the departed.[2]

We need no fanciful hypotheses to explain the reason and designate the time of these constructions. The bare recountal of the burial rites that prevailed

[1] Archæologia Americana, Vol. I.

[2] On the *rôle* of trees in primitive religions consult Guigniaut, Religions de l'Antiquitè, T. I., pp. 81, 150, note, 391, 406.

among the aborigines is all sufficient to solve the riddle of bone-mounds both as they occur in Florida and all other States. The great feature of these rites was to preserve the bones of the dead, a custom full of significance in nature-worship everywhere. For this purpose the corpses were either exposed or buried till sufficient decomposition had ensued to permit the flesh to be easily removed. The bones were then scraped clean, and either carried to private dwellings, or deposited in public charnel-houses; such were the "Templos que servian de Entierros y no de Casas de Oracion," seen by De Soto at Tampa Bay,[1] and the "Osarios," bone-houses, in Cofachiqui, among the Cherokees.[2] Finally, at stated periods, they were collected from all quarters, deposited in some predetermined spot, and there covered with soil heaped into the shape of a cone. Annual additions to the same cemetery gave rise to the extraordinary dimensions that some attained; or several interments were made near the same spot, and hence the groups often seen.[3]

As the Natchez, Taencas, and other southern tribes were accustomed to place the council-house and chief's dwelling on artificial elevations, both to give them an air of superior dignity, to render them easy of defence,

[1] La Vega, Conq. de la Florida, Lib. I., cap. IV., p. 5.

[2] Ibid. Lib. III., cap XIV., p. 129, cap. XV., p. 131, et sq.

[3] For descriptions of this mode of interment, essentially the same in most of the tribes from the Mississippi to the St. Lawrence, and very widely prevalent in South America, consult Wm. Bartram, Travels, p. 516; Romans, Nat. Hist. Fla., pp. 88–90; Adair, Hist. N. Am. Inds., p 183; Lawson, New Account of Carolina, p. 182, in Stevens' Collection; Beverly, Hist. de la Virginie, pp. 259–62; Baumgarten, Ges. von Amerika, B. I., s. 470; Colden, Hist. of the Five Nations, p. 16, and many others.

and in some localities to protect from inundations,[1] so the natives of Florida, in pursuance of the same custom, either erected such tumuli for this purpose, or more probably, only took advantage of those burial mounds that the vicissitudes of war had thrown in their hands, or a long period of time deprived of sacred associations. In the town of Ucita, where De Soto landed, "The Lordes house stoode neere the shore upon a very hie mounte made by hande for strength,"[2] and La Vega gives in detail their construction.

While this examination of their sepulchral rites, taken in connection with the discovery of glass beads *in situ*, leaves no doubt but that such remains were the work of the people who inhabited the peninsula at its discovery by Europeans, it is not probable that the custom was retained much after this period. The Lower Creeks and Seminoles, so far from treating their dead thus, took pains to conceal the graves, and never erected mounds save in one emergency. This was in the event of a victorious battle, when they collected the dead into one vast pile, and covered them with earth,[3] simply because it was the most convenient way to pay those last and mournful duties that humanity demands at our hands.

Another class of burial mounds, tallying very nearly with those said by the French to have been raised over their dead by the early Indians of the St. Johns, are not unusual in the hammocks along this river. They

[1] See an instructive notice from Pere le Petit in the Lettres Edifiantes et Curieuses, T. IV., pp. 261–2, and the Inca, Lib. II., pp. 69–70; Lib. IV., p. 188; Lib. V., pp. 202, 231, &c.

[2] Port. Gent., in Hackluyt, V., p. 489.

[3] Nar. of Oceola Nikkanoche, pp. 71–2. The author speaks of one "that must have covered two acres of ground," but this is probably a misapprehension.

are only a few feet in height, resembling in appearance the hillocks of humus left by the roots of uprooted trees, from which they can be distinguished by their general range, (N., S.,) by the hollows on each side whence the earth was obtained, and by their construction. They are sometimes distinctly stratified, presenting layers of sand, ashes and charcoal, and clay. Bones, arrow-heads, axes, and pottery are found in them, but as far as my own observations extended, and those of a Norwegian settler bearing the classic name of Ivon Ericson, who assured me he had examined them frequently on the Upper St. Johns, in no case were beads or other articles indicating a familiarity with European productions discovered.

The utensils, the implements of war and the chase exhumed from the mounds, and found in their vicinity, do not differ from those in general use among the Indians of all parts at their first discovery,[1] and go to corroborate the opinion that all these earthworks—and I am inclined to assert the same of the whole of those in the other Atlantic States, and the majority in the Mississippi valley—were the production, not of some mythical tribe of high civilization in remote antiquity, but of the identical nations found by the whites residing in these regions.

An equally interesting and more generally distributed class of antiquities are the beds and heaps of

[1] I am aware that Mr. Schoolcraft places the pottery of Florida intermediate between the coarse work of the northern hunter tribes, and the almost artistic manufactures of Yucatan and Mexico, (see an article on the Antiquities of Florida, in the Hist. of the Ind. Tribes, Vol. III.;) but the numerous specimens obtained in various parts of the peninsula that I had opportunities to examine, never seemed to indicate a civilization so advanced.

shells. These are found with more or less frequency on the shores of every State from Connecticut southward along the Atlantic and Gulf of Mexico. Some of them are of enormous extent, covering acres of ground, and of a singular height. For a long time it was a debateable point whether they belonged to the domain of the geologist or antiquarian; later researches have awarded them to both, by distinguishing between those of natural and artificial origin.[1] The latter are recognized by the presence of darts, pottery, charcoal, &c., in *original connection* with the shells and debris throughout the mass, by the presence of surface soil, roots, and stumps, *in situ* beneath the heap, by nearness to an open fishing shore, and finally by the valves of the shell fish being asunder and their edges factured or burnt; on the other hand, whole closed shells as at Easton in Maryland, fragments of older fossils in original connection, distinct stratification,[2] and remoteness from any known oyster bed, as those of northern Texas, northern Georgia, and perhaps of Cumberland county, New Jersey, are convincing proofs of their natural deposition.

Examples in Florida are numerous and striking. At Fernandina new town on Amelia island, a layer extends along the face of the bluff for one hundred and fifty yards and inland a quarter of a mile, sometimes three feet in depth, composed almost wholly of shells of the esculent oyster though with clams and conches sparsely intermixed. The valves are all separate, the

[1] There is an excellent paper on this topic by the well-known geologist, Lardner Vanuxem, in the Trans. Am. Assoc. Geol. and Naturalists, for 1840–42, p. 21. sq.

[2] This is not an invariable proof however; see Tuomey, Geol. Survey of S. Car., p. 199, note.

shells in some places rotten, fractured and mixed with sand, charcoal, and pottery, while in others as clean and sound as if just from the hands of the oysterman.

Similar deposits are found in various parts of the island; on the main land opposite; on both sides of the entrance to the St. Johns; on Anastasia island; and every where along the coast both of the Atlantic and the Gulf. One of the most remarkable is Turtle Mound on Musquito Lagoon, near New Smyrna. "It is thirty feet high, composed almost altogether of separate oyster shells, it being rare to find an entire one; there are also some conch and clam shells, both of which are, however, exceedingly scarce. That it is artificial there is no doubt on my mind. Some eight or ten years since we experienced a gale in this section of the country, from the northwest, which caused that portion of the mound facing the river, the steepest part, to wash and fall considerably; being there a few days afterwards, I took considerable pains to examine the face of it, and found as low as the bottom and as high up as I could observe, numberless pieces of Indian pottery, and quantities of bones principally of fish, but no human ones; also charcoal and beds of ashes. The one on which I reside, opposite New Smyrna, is precisely of the same formation. Having had occasion some time back to dig a hole six or eight feet deep, I found precisely the same contents that I have described at Turtle Mound, with the addition of some few flint arrowheads."

For this interesting description from the pen of a gentleman of the vicinity I am indebted to the kindness of Mr. F. L. Dancy, State Geologist of Florida; he adds from his own observation an account of one on Chrystal river, on the Gulf coast, four miles from its mouth. "The marsh of the river at that point is some twenty yards wide to the firm land, at which point this mound commences to rise; it is on all sides nearly perpendicular, the faces covered with brush and trees to which the curious have to cling to effect an ascent. It is about forty feet in height, the top surface nearly level, about thirty feet across, and covered with magnolia, live-oak, and other forest trees, some of them four feet in diameter. Its form is that of a truncated cone, and as far as can be judged from external appearance, it is composed exclusively of oyster shells and vegetable mould. These shells are all separated. The mound was evidently thrown up by the Indians for a lookout, as the Gulf can be distinctly seen from its summit. There are no oysters growing at this time within four or five miles of it."

Other shell heaps are met with along the coast but none equalling in magnitude that seen by Sir Charles Lyell[1] on Cannon's Island at the mouth of the Altamaha, covering ten acres of ground, "elevated in some places ten feet and on an average five feet above the general level," and which this eminent geologist attributes exclusively to the Indians, or the vast beds of *Gnathodon Cuneatus*, on Mobile Bay, described by Mr. Hale,[2] which, however, are probably of natural formation, though containing quantities of human bones, pottery, images, &c.

It is strange that we find no notices of the formation of these heaps by the early travellers; I do not remember to have met with any except a line in Cabeza de Vaca, where, speaking of a tribe on the Gulf, he

[1] Second Visit to the United States, Vol. I., p. 252.
[2] Am. Jour. of Science, Vol. XI., (2 ser.) pp. 164–74.

says their houses were "built of mats on heaps of oyster shells."[1]

Along Manatee river I noticed numerous small heaps of conches, attributable to the later Indians, and in the post-pliocene shellbluffs at the mouth of this river, nearly twenty feet in height composed largely of a species of *Pyrula*,[2] I found numerous fragments of a coarse, ill-marked, pottery, not, however, where the shells were unbroken and clean, but where they were fragmentary, mixed with charcoal, ashes and dirt, and never more than three feet below the surface. The singular hillocks, whose formation is a geological enigma not readily solved, so frequent along the St. Johns, vast aggregations of Helices with some Unios and other fresh water shells in connection, without admixture of earth, in some cases thirty feet high, and irregularly stratified, are not to be mistaken for those of artificial construction, though from the frequency of Indian relics found in them, they seem to have been a chosen place of burial for the aboriginal tribes.

Among the relics dating from a later period are the "Indian Old Fields." These are portions of land once cleared and cultivated by the Seminoles, and are found wherever the fertility of the soil promised favorably for agriculture. They are very abundant in Alachua, where, says Bartram,[3] "almost every step dis-

[1] Le case loro sono edificate di stuore sopra scorze d'ostriche, e sopra di esse dormono sopra cuoi d'animali. Relatione que fece Alvaro Nunez, detto Capo di Vaca, Ramusio, Viaggi, T. III., fol. 317., E.

[2] On the geology of these bluffs, see the articles by Mr. Allen, in the first, and Mr. Conrad in the second volume of the Am. Jour. Science. (Second series.)

[3] Travels, p. 198.

covers traces of ancient human habitation," reminding us of the time "when the Indians could assemble by thousands at ball play and other juvenile diversions and athletic exercises on these then happy fields and green plains." Such is the tenacity of the soil for retaining impressions, that the marks of tillage by which these are distinguished from the Spanish old fields are easily seen and readily discriminated, even after they are covered by a dense growth of trees.

APPENDIX I.

THE SILVER SPRING.

THE geological formation of Florida gives rise to springs and fountains of such magnitude and beauty, that they deserve to be ranked with the great fresh-water lakes, the falls of Niagara, and the Mississippi river, as grand hydrographical features of the North American continent. The most remarkable are the Wakulla, twelve miles from Tallahassie, of great depth and an icy coldness, which is the best known, and has been described by the competent pen of Castlenau and others, the Silver Spring and the Manatee Spring. The latter is on the left bank of the Suwannee, forty-five miles from its mouth, and is so named from having been a favorite haunt of the sea-cow, (*Trichechus Manatus,*) whose bones, discolored by the sulphuret of iron held in solution by the water, are still found there.

The Silver Spring, in some respects the most remarkable of the three, is in the centre of Marion county, ten miles from the Ocklewaha, into which its stream flows, and six miles from Ocala, the county seat. In December, 1856, I had an opportunity to examine it with the aid of proper instruments, which I did with much care. It has often been visited as a natural curiosity, and is considered by tourists one of the lions of the

State. To be appreciated in its full beauty, it should be approached from the Ocklewaha. For more than a week I had been tediously ascending this river in a pole-barge, wearied with the monotony of the dank and gloomy forests that everywhere shade its inky stream,[1] when one bright morning a sharp turn brought us into the pellucid waters of the Silver Spring Run. A few vigorous strokes and we had left behind us the cypress swamps and emerged into broad, level savannas, that stretched miles away on either hand to the far-off pine woods that, like a frame, shut in the scene. In the summer season these prairies, clothed in the luxuriance of a tropical vegetation, gorgeously decked with

[1] The peculiar hue of the whole St. Johns system of streams has been termed by various travellers a light brown, light red, coffee color, rich umber, and beer color. In the sun it is that of a weak lye, but in the shade often looks as black as ink. The water is quite translucent and deposits no sediment. The same phenomenon is observed in the low country of Carolina, New Jersey, and Lake Superior, and on a large scale in the Rio Negro, Atababo. Temi, and others of South America. In the latter, Humboldt (Ansichten der Natur, B. I., p. 263–4) ascribes it "to a solution of carburetted hydrogen, to the luxuriance of a tropical vegetation, and to the quantity of plants and herbs on the ground on which they flow." In Florida, the vast marshes and hammocks, covered the year round with water from a few inches to two feet in depth, yet producing such rank vegetation as to block up the rivers with floating islands, are doubtless the main cause. The Hillsboro, Suwannee, and others, flowing through the limestone lands into the Gulf, are on the other hand remarkable for the clarity of their streams. I have drank this natural decoction when it tasted and smelt so strongly of decayed vegetable matter as almost to induce nausea. A fact not readily explained is that while the dark waters of other regions are marked by a lack of fish and crocodiles, a freedom from stinging musquitoes, a cooler atmosphere and greater salubrity, nothing of the kind occurs on these streams.

innumerable flowers, and alive with countless birds and insects of brilliant hues, offer a spectacle that once seen can never be forgotten.

But far more strangely beautiful than the scenery around is that beneath—the subaqueous landscape. At times the bottom is clothed in dark-green sedge waving its long tresses to and fro in the current, now we pass over a sunken log draperied in delicate aquatic moss thick as ivy, again the scene changes and a bottom of greyish sand throws in bright relief concentric arcs of brilliantly white fragments of shells deposited on the lower side of ripple marks in a circular basin. Far below us, though apparently close at hand, enormous trout dash upon their prey or patiently lie in wait undisturbed by the splash of the poles and the shouts of the negroes, huge cat-fish rest sluggishly on the mud, and here and there, every protuberance and bony ridge distinctly visible, the dark form of an alligator is distended on the bottom or slowly paddles up the stream. Thus for ten miles of an almost straight course, east and west, is the voyager continually surprised with fresh beauties and unimagined novelties.

The width of the stream varies from sixty to one hundred and twenty-five feet, its average greatest depth about twenty, the current always quite rapid. For about one mile below its head, forests of cypress, maple, ash, gum, and palmetto adorn the banks with a pleasing variety of foliage. The basin itself is somewhat elliptical in form, the exit being at the middle of one side; its transverse diameter measures about one hundred and fifty yards, (N. E., S. W.,) its conjugate one hundred yards. Easterly it is bordered by a cypress swamp, while the opposite bank is hidden by a dense, wet hammock. A few yards from the brink opposite the exit runs a limestone ridge of moderate elevation covered with pine and jack-oak.

The principal entrance of the water is at the north-eastern extremity. Here a subaqueous limestone bluff presents three craggy ledges, between the undermost of which and the base is an orifice, about fifteen feet in length by five in height, whence the water gushes with great violence. Another and smaller entrance is at the opposite extremity. The maximum depth was at the time of my visit forty-one feet. The water is tasteless, presents no signs of mineral matter in solution, and so perfectly diaphanous that the smallest shell is entirely visible on the bottom of the deepest portion. Slowly drifting in a canoe over the precipice I could not restrain an involuntary start of terror, so difficult was it, from the transparency of the supporting medium for the mind to appreciate its existence. When the sun-beams fall full upon the water, by a familiar optical delusion, it seems to a spectator on the bank that the bottom and sides of the basin are elevated, and over the whole, over the frowning crags, the snow-white shells, the long sedge, and the moving aquatic tribes, the decomposed light flings its rainbow hues, and all things float in a sea of colors, magnificent and impressive beyond description. What wonder that the untaught children of nature spread the fame of this marvellous fountain to far distant climes, and under the stereoscopic power of time and distance came to regard it as the life-giving stream, whose magic waters washed away the calamities of age and the pains of disease, round whose fortunate shores youths and maidens ever sported, eternally young and eternally joyous!

During my stay I took great pains to ascertain the

exact temperature of the water and from a number of observations made at various hours of the day obtained a constant result of 73.2°, Fahrenheit. This is higher than the mean annual temperature of the locality, which, as determined by a thermometrical record kept at Fort King near Ocala for six years, is 70.00°; while it is lower than that of the small mineral springs so abundant throughout the peninsula, which I rarely found less than 75°. It is probable, however, that this is not a fixed temperature but varies with the amount of water thrown out. Competent observers, resident on the spot, informed me that a variation of three feet in the vertical depth of the basin had been known to occur in one year, though this was far greater than usual. The time of highest water is shortly after the rainy season, about the month of September, a fact that indicates the cause of the change.

Visiting the spring when at a medium height I enjoyed peculiar advantages for calculating the amount of water given forth. The method I used was the convenient and sufficiently accurate one of the log and line, the former of three inches radius, the latter one hundred and two feet in length. In estimating the size of the bed I chose a point about a quarter of a mile from the basin. The results were calculated according to the formulæ of Buat. After making all possible allowance for friction, for imperfection of instruments, and inaccuracy of observation, the average daily quantity of water thrown out by this single spring reaches the enormous amount of more than three hundred million gallons!

Numbers such as this are beyond the grasp of the human intellect, bewildering rather than enlightening the mind. Let us take another unit and compare it with the most stupendous hydrographical works of man that have been the wonders of the world. Most renowned of these are the aqueducts of Rome. In the latter half of the first century, when Frontinus was inspector, the public register indicated a daily supply of fourteen thousand and eighteen quinaria, about one hundred and ninety-six million gallons. Or we can choose modern instances. The city of London is said to require forty million gallons every twenty-four hours, New York about one-third, and Philadelphia one-quarter as much. Thus we see that this one fount furnishes more than enough water to have satisfied the wants of Rome in her most imperial days, to supply plenteously eight cities as large as London, a score of New Yorks, or thirty Philadelphias. By the side of its stream the far-famed aqueduct of Lyons, yielding one million two hundred and nine thousand six hundred gallons daily, or the Croton aqueduct, whose maximum diurnal capacity is sixty million gallons, seems of feeble importance, while the stateliest canals of Solomon, Theodoric, or the Ptolemies dwindle to insignificant rivulets.

Neither is this the emergence of a sunken river as is the case with the Wakulla fountain, but is a spring in the strictest sense of the word, deriving its sustenance from the rains that percolate the porous tertiary limestone that forms the central ridge of the peninsula.

There are many other springs both saline, mineral, and of pure water, which would be looked upon as wonders in any country where such wonders were less abundant. Such are the Six Mile Spring (White Spring, Silver Spring), and the Salt Spring on the western shore of Lake George, a sulphur spring on

Lake Monroe, one mile from Enterprise, another eight miles from Tampa on the Hillsboro' river, Gadsden's spring in Columbia county, the Blue spring on the Ocklawaha, Orange Springs in Alachua county, the Oakhumke the source of the Withlacooche, and numberless others of less note.[1] Besides these, the other hydrographical features of the peninsula are unique and instructive, well deserving a thorough and special examination; such are the intermittent lakes, which, like the famous Lake Kauten in Prussia, the Lugea Palus or Zirchnitzer See in the duchy of Carniola, and the classical Lake Fucinus, have their regular periods of annual ebb and flow; while the sinking rivers Santa Fe, Chipola, Econfinna, Ocilla and others offer no less interesting objects of study than their analogues in the secondary limestone of Styria, in Istria, Carniola, Cuba, and other regions.

When we ponder on the cause of these phenomena we are led to the most extraordinary conclusions. To explain them we are obliged to accept the opinion—which very many associated facts tend to substantiate—that the lower strata of the limestone formation of the peninsula have been hollowed out by the action of water into vast subterranean reservoirs, into enormous caverns that intersect and ramify, extending in some cases far under the bed of the adjacent ocean, through whose sunless corridors roll nameless rivers, and in whose sombre halls sleep black lakes. During the rainy season, gathering power in silence deep in the bowels of the earth, they either expend it quietly in

[1] For particulars concerning some of these, see Wm. Bartram, Travels, pp. 145, 165, 206, 230; Notices of E. Florida, by a recent Trav., pp. 28, 44; American Journal of Science, Vol. XXV., p. 165, I, (2 ser.) p. 39.

fountains of surprising magnitude, or else, bursting forth in violent eruptions, rend asunder the overlying strata, forming the "lime sinks," and "bottomless lakes," common in many counties of Florida; or should this occur beneath the ocean, causing the phenomenon of "freshening," sometimes to such an extent as to afford drinkable water miles from land, as occurred some years ago off Anastasia Island, and in January, 1857, near Key West.

APPENDIX II.

THE MUMMIES OF THE MISSISSIPPI VALLEY.

A NUMBER of years ago considerable curiosity was excited by the discovery of mummies in Tennessee and Kentucky, and many theories were promulged regarding their origin, but I believe neither that nor their age has, as yet, been satisfactorily determined.

Some were found as early as 1775, near Lexington, Kentucky, but we have no definite account of any before those exhumed September 2, 1810, in a copperas cave in Warren county, Tennessee, on the Cany fork of the Cumberland river, ten miles below the Falls. These were described in the Medical Repository by Mr. Miller, whose article was followed by another in the same periodical, illustrated by a sketch, in support of the view that this discovery indicated the derivation of the Indians from the Malays and Tartars. The same pair was also described by Breckenridge and Flint a few years later.

Shortly previous to 1813, two mummies were found in the Gothic avenue of the Mammoth Cave, and not long afterwards, (1814,) another in the Audabon avenue.

The same year, several more were discovered in a nitre cave near Glasgow, Kentucky, by Thomas Monroe, who forwarded one to the American Antiquarian Society, described by Dr. Mitchell in the first volume of the publications of that body.

Again, in 1828, two more were found in a complete state of preservation in a cave of West Tennessee, mentioned in the American Journal of Science, (Vol. xxii. p. 124.)

With that zest for the wonderful, for which antiquarians are somewhat famous, the idea that these remains could belong to tribes with whom the first settlers were acquainted, was rejected, and recourse was had to Malays, South Sea Islanders, and the antipodes generally, for a more *reasonable* explanation. It was said that the envelopes of the bodies (all of which bore close resemblance among themselves) pointed to a higher state of the arts than existed among the Indians of the Mississippi Valley, and that the physical differences, the color of the hair, &c., were irreconcileable. I think, however, it may be shown that these objections are of no weight, and that the bodies in question were interred at a comparatively late period.

The wrappings consisted usually of deer skins, dressed and undressed, mats of split canes, some as much as sixty yards long, and a woven stuff called "blankets," "sheets," and "cloth;" this was often either bordered with feathers of the wild turkey and other birds, or covered with them in squares and patterns. Their ages, as guessed from appearances, varied from ten years to advanced life. In several cases the mark of a severe blow on the head was seen, which must have caused the individual's death. Their stature was usually in conformity to their supposed age;[1] the weight of one, as given by Flint, six or eight pounds; in all cases but one the hair of a "sorrel," "foxy," "yellow" or "sandy" color; and they were usually found five or six feet below the surface.

First, then, in our examination, the question arises, did the Indians of the Mississippi Valley, when first met by the whites, possess the art of manufacturing woven stuff of the kind mentioned? In answer we have the express words of the Inca,[2] "These mantles the Indians of Florida make of a certain herb-like mallows, (malvas,) which has fibres like flax, (que tiene hebra, como lino,) and from the same they make thread, to which they give colors which remain most firmly." The next explorer was La Salle; in Tonty's account of his expedition,[3] he remarks that he saw in a council lodge of the Taencas, "sixty old men clothed in large white cloaks, which are made by the women from the bark of the mulberry tree." Still more to our purpose are the words of later writers, who mention the interweaving of feathers. Not only, says Dumont,[4] do the Indian women make garters and ribbons of the wool of the buffalo, (du laine du beuf,) but also a sort of mat of threads obtained from the bark of the linden, (tilleul,) "qu'elles couvrent de plumes de cigne des plus fines, attachèes une à une

1 Flint, (Travels, Let. XVI., p. 172,) says that neither of those found in 1810 measured more than four feet. This is an error. He only saw the female, whose age was not over fourteen, and the squatting position in which the body was, deceived him.

2 Conq. de la Florida, Lib. V., P. II., cap. VIII.

3 In French's Hist. Coll. of La., Pt. I., p. 61.

4 Mems. Hist. sur la Louisiane, T. I., pp 154-5.

ur cet toil." Dupratz[1] mentions similar cloaks of mulberry bark covered "with the feathers of swans, turkeys, and India ducks," the fibres of the bark being twisted "about the thickness of packthread," and woven "with a wrought border around the edges." Of the Indians of North Carolina, Lawson says,[2] "Their feather match-coats are very pretty, especially some of them which are made extraordinary charming, containing several pretty figures, wrought in feathers, making them seem like a fine flower Silk-Shag." Other examples might be given, but these are sufficient.

The cane mat was an article of daily use among the tribes wherever the cane grew, and was bartered to those where it did not. The Arkanzas, Taencas, Cenis, Natchez, and Gulf tribes, used it to cover their huts;[3] hence a piece even sixty yards long was no uncommon matter; while in one instance at least,[4] we know that the eastern tribes rolled their dead in them, tying them fast at both ends. All the minor articles of ornament and dress, the bone and horn needles, the vegetable beads, &c., can be shown with equal facility to have been in general use among the natives.[5]

It has usually been supposed that these bodies were preserved by the chemical action of the nitriferous soil around them; but this does not account for their per-

[1] Hist. of Louisiana, Vol. II., p. 230.

[2] A New Account of Carolina, p. 191.

[3] Joutel, Jour. Hist., p. 218; Mems. of Sieur de Tonty, p. 61; Dupratz, V. II., p. 22; Cabeza de Vaca. in Ramusio, T. III., fol. 317, E.

[4] Lawson, ubi suprà, p. 180.

[5] It was remarked of the mummy found in the Mammoth cave, "In the making of her dress there is no evidence of the use of any other machinery than bone and horn needles." (Collin's Kentucky, p. 257.)

fection and extreme desiccation, inclosed as they were in such voluminous envelopes. Yet it is quite certain that the viscera were never absent, nor has any balm or gum been found upon them.[1] Hence, if artificially prepared, it must have been by protracted drying by fire, in a manner common among the ancient inhabitants of the Caroline islands, the Tahitians, the Guanches of Teneriffe, and still retained in some convents in the Levant. It is well known that in America the Popayans, the Nicaraguans, and the Caribs of the West Indies had this custom;[2] but I believe that attention has not been called to the fact, that this very mode of preserving the dead was used more or less by the Indians of the Mississippi Valley. The southern tribes of Mississippi and Alabama dried the corpse of their chief over a slow fire, placed it in the temple as an object of adoration till the death of his successor, and then transferred it to the bottom or cellar (fond) of the building.[3] Analogous usages, modifications of this and probably derived from it, prevailed among the tribes of North Carolina, Virginia, and the Pacific coast,[4] while we have seen that Bristock asserts the same of the Apalachites. That a cave should be substituted for a temple, or that the bodies should be ultimately inhumed, cannot excite our surprise when we recall how subject the Indians

[1] Archæologia Americana, Vol. I., p. 230.

[2] Whence the French verb *boucaner*, and the English *buccaneer*. Possibly the custom may have been introduced among the tribes of the northern shore of the Gulf by the Caribs.

[3] Dumont, Mems., Hist. sur la Louisiane, T. I, p. 240.

[4] De Bry, Peregrinationes in America, P. I., Tab. XXII.: Beverly, Hist. de la Virginie, Liv. III., pp. 285–6; Lawson, Acc't of Carolina, p. 182; Schoolcraft, Hist. Ind. Tribes, Vol. V., p 693.

were to sudden attacks, how solicitous that their dead should not be disturbed,[1] and how caves were ever regarded by them as natural temples for their gods and most fit resting places for their dead.[2]

The rarity of the mummies may be easily accounted for as only the bodies of the chiefs were thus preserved. Yet it is a significant fact that a body is rarely, if ever, found alone. Moreover, in every case of which we have special description, these are of different sexes, and one, the female, and the youngest, sometimes apparently not more than twelve or fourteen years of age, evidently died by violence. How readily these seemingly unconnected facts take place and order, and how intelligible they become, when we learn that at the death of a ruler the Indians sacrificed and buried with him one or two of his wives, and in some tribes the youngest was always the chosen victim of this cruel superstition.[3]

The light color of the hair is doubtless caused by the nitriferous soil with which it had been so long surrounded; a supposition certified by one instance, where, in consequence of the unusually voluminous wrappings, and perhaps a later interment, it retained the black color of that of the true Indian.[4]

Though most of these references relate to nations not dwelling immediately in the area of country where

[1] See the Inca, Lib. IV., caps. VIII., IX.

[2] See the Am. Jour. of Science, Vol. I., p. 429; Vol. XXII., p. 124; Collin's Kentucky, pp. 177, 448, 520, 541; Bradford, Am. Antiqs., Pt. I. p. 29.

[3] Dumont, Mems. Hist., T. II., pp. 178, 238; Dupratz, Vol. II., p. 221, and for the latter fact, Mems. of the Sieur de Tonty, p. 61.

[4] Medical Repository, Vol. XVI., p. 148. This opinion is endorsed by Bradford, Am. Antiqs., p. 31.

the mummies are found, it is quite unnecessary for me to refer in this connection to those numerous and valid arguments, derived both from tradition and archæology, that prove beyond doubt that this tract, and indeed the whole Ohio valley, had changed masters shortly before the whites explored it, and that its former possessors when not destroyed by the invaders, had been driven south.

Hence we may reasonably infer, that as no article found upon the mummies indicates a higher degree of art than was possessed by the southern Indians, as the physical changes are owing to casual *post mortem* circumstances, as we have positive authority that certain tribes were accustomed to preserve the corpses of their chiefs; and lastly, as we have many evidences to show that such tribes, or those closely associated with with them, once dwelt further north than they were first found, consequently the deposition of the mummies must be ascribed to a race who dwelt near the region where they occur, at the time of its exploration by Europeans.

APPENDIX III.

THE PRECIOUS METALS POSSESSED BY THE EARLY FLORIDIAN INDIANS.

THE main idea that inspired the Spanish expeditions to Florida was the hope of discovering riches there, equal to the gorgeous opulence of Peru and Mexico. Although the country was supposed to be north of the auriferous zone—in accordance with which geological notion in his map of the world (1529) Diego de Ribero inscribes on the land marked "Tierra de Garay," north of the Gulf of Mexico, now West Florida, "This land is poor in gold, as it lies too far from the tropic of Cancer"[1]—yet an abiding faith in its riches was kept alive by Spanish traders obtaining from time to time morsels of gold from the natives. As early as the first voyage of De Leon (1512), they possessed and used it as an article of barter in small quantities.[2] The later explorers, Narvaez, De Soto, Ribaut, and

[1] Humboldt, Krit. Untersuch. ueber die Hist. Entwickelung der Geog. Kentnisse der neuen Welt, B. I., s. 322; the same reason is given by De Laet, Descrip. Ind. Occident. Lib. IV., cap. XIV.

[2] "Guañines de oro," Navarrete, Viages, Tom. III., p. 52; Herrera, Dec. I., Lib. IX., cap. XI.

Laudonniére, report both gold and silver, but never, as far as their own observations went, in any abundance. The savages were always eagerly questioned as to its origin and always returned one of two answers; either that they had pilfered it from the wrecks of vessels driven on their coasts, or else they referred the inquirer to a distant and mountainous country to the north, known both to the nations on the Gulf of Mexico, those at the extreme south of the peninsula, and those on the Atlantic coast as far north as the Savannah river, as Apalache. Here, said the rumors, the men wore cuirasses of gold and shields of burnished silver, while the women were impeded in their dancing by the weight of their golden ornaments and strings of pearls. We have seen that this name was at one period applied to a large area of country, and hence have no difficulty in appreciating the error that Narvaez committed when he supposed the small town of that name east of the Apalachicola to contain the major part of the nation. Fontanedo, whose long residence among the Indians renders him one of our best authorities on certain points, says expressly that the snowy mountains of Onagatano whence the gold was obtained were the *furthermost possessions of Apalache.*[1]

There is a general similarity in the accounts of the direction and remoteness of the mines. The coast tribes north of the St. Johns river had pieces of *sieroa pira,* red metal, which was tested by a goldsmith who accompanied Laudonniére and found to be pure gold. When asked where this was obtained they pointed to the north. Another chief who gave them slips of sil-

[1] Mais on n'y trouve pas d'or, parce qu'elle est eloignè des mines d'Onagatono, situées dans les montagnes neigeuses d'Onagatono dernieres possessions d'Abolachi, Memoire, p. 32.

ver said it came from a country at the foot of lofty mountains ten long days' journey inland, towards the north. A third had small grains of gold, silver, and copper, procured, according to his own account, by washing the sands of a creek that flowed at the base of lofty mountains five or six days journey in a north-westerly direction. The artist Le Moyne de Morgues, drawing somewhat on his imagination, represents in his forty-first sketch this method of cleaning it. Hence on some maps of a very early period the southern Alleghanies bear the name *Apalatcy Montes Auriferi.* Years afterwards, rumors derived from the Indians were rife among the Spanish colonists of a "very rich and exceeding great city, called La Grand Copal, among the mountains of Gold and Chrystal," fifteen or twenty days journey northwest of St. Augustine.[1]

Now as the gold mines of Georgia and Carolina lie about three hundred miles north or northwest of Florida, such accounts as these can leave no reasonable doubt but that they were known to the Indians, and to a certain extent worked before the arrival of the white man. Indeed, may we not impute to them the ancient and unrecorded mining operations, signs of which are occasionally met with in the gold country of Georgia? Such are the remains of what are called "furnaces," the marks of excavations, various rude metallurgical instruments, the buried log houses, and other tokens of a large population in some remote past, found from time to time in the vicinity of Dahlonega and various parts of the Nacooche valley.[2] These

[1] Pedro Morales, in Hackluyt, Vol. III., p. 432.

[2] See Lanman's Letters from the Allegheny Mountains, pp. 9, 26, 27; White, Hist. Coll. of Georgia, pp. 487–8.

were referred by the finders to De Soto, who offers a favorite and ready explanation for any construction of unknown age, in that part of our country; thus I have been told that the bone mounds in Florida were the burial places of his soldiers, and on one occasion a post pliocene bank of shells on Tampa Bay was pointed out to me as the ruins of one of his forts. It is unnecessary to add that the soldiers under this ill-fated leader spent no time in digging gold either in north Georgia or anywhere else.

That in the course of barter small quantities of the metals here obtained—for we must ascribe to shipwrecks the "lumps of gold several pounds in weight" said to have been found in modern times on the shores of Florida and Carolina[1]—should have gradually proceeded to the nations on the shores of the Atlantic and the Gulf of Mexico, and even to the Caloosas in South Florida, four hundred miles from their starting point, will not astonish any one acquainted with the extent to which the transportation of metals was carried by the aborigines in other portions of the continent.

[1] Humboldt, Island of Cuba, p. 131, note.

END.

ACADEMY OF SCIENCES.

At the regular meeting of the Academy of Sciences last evening, Mr. William Bross delivered an address on the region of the Canadian Pacific Railroad. He said that British Columbia, for a distance of 1,000 or 1,500 miles north of the United States border, was a magnificent wheat country. The climate was modified by the Japan stream in the Pacific Ocean, and was much warmer than other places in that latitude. The country was filling up with great rapidity along the railroad, 400 miles of which were built in one year. He had seen a town there of 3,500 inhabitants which was only two years old. Beyond Manitoba no liquor was allowed. The red-coats entered the trains and made a search for bottles of whisky. The result was great sobriety, thrift, and good order in the regions beyond. Dr. S. R. Haven gave an interesting account of a visit he paid lately to the western coast of Florida, and of some of his explorations in the prehistoric mounds of that country. He found many human skulls, and a large proportion of them were perforated on the back part. He subsequently found similar perforations in the conch-shells of the shell-mounds. The holes in the shells, it is thought were made by the Indians, so that they could blow the conch out and eat it. This suggested to him the theory that the perforated skulls were the skulls of people who had been burned at the stake, and that the holes were made in them so that the cooked brains could be blown out and eaten by the cannibal Indians. Dr. George W. Mason, of Bloomington, gave a brief address of an ancient forest that had been discovered in a coal shaft in McLean County, 170 feet below the surface. It was voted that a meeting be held two weeks hence to hear a lecture from Dr. Edward Andrews, after which the academy adjourned.

www.ingramcontent.com/pod-product-compliance
Lightning Source LLC
LaVergne TN
LVHW011217110826
845150LV00006B/1450